Aberdeen *and* Royal Deeside

WALKS

Compiled by
Brian Conduit

JARROLD

Acknowledgements
My thanks for the valuable advice and numerous useful leaflets that I obtained from the various tourist information centres throughout the area.

Text:	Brian Conduit
Photography:	Brian Conduit
Editors:	Sarah Letts
Designers:	Brian Skinner, Doug Whitworth
Mapping:	Heather Pearson

Series Consultant: Brian Conduit

Jarrold Publishing 0-7117-1595-5

While every care has been taken to ensure the accuracy of the route directions, the publishers cannot accept responsibility for errors or omissions, or for changes in details given. The countryside is not static: hedges and fences can be removed, field boundaries can alter, footpaths can be rerouted and changes in ownership can result in the closure or diversion of some concessionary paths. Also, paths that are easy and pleasant for walking in fine conditions may become slippery, muddy and difficult in wet weather, while stepping stones across rivers and streams may become impassable.

If you find an inaccuracy in either the text or the maps, please write to or email Jarrold Publishing at the addresses below.

First published 2001
by Jarrold Publishing

Printed in Belgium
by Proost NV, Turnhout. 1/01

Jarrold Publishing,
Pathfinder Guides, Whitefriars, Norwich NR3 1TR
E-mail: pathfinder@jarrold.com

Front cover:	BRAEMAR CASTLE
Previous page:	DUFF HOUSE

Contents

Short, easy walks

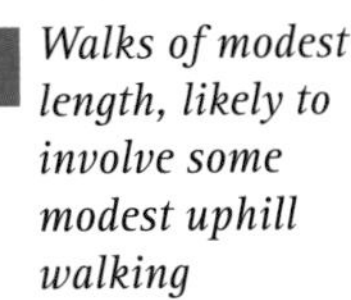

Walks of modest length, likely to involve some modest uphill walking

More challenging walks which may be longer and/or over more rugged terrain, often with some stiff climbs

Keymap 1

SCALE 1:400 000 or 1 INCH to 6.4 MILES 1CM to 4KM
0 2 4 6 8 10 KILOMETRES 15
0 2 4 6 MILES 8 10
Halliman Skerries
LOSSIEMOUTH
Boar's Head Rock
SPEY BAY
FINDOCHTY
PORTKNOCKIE
BUCKIE
CULLEN
Logie Head
Redhythe Point
PORTSOY
ELGIN
20
7
Bin of Cullen
Shiel Muir
Aultmore
Teindland
Wood of Ordiequish
Millstone Hill
KEITH
ROTHES
Ben Aigan
Hill of Towie
STRATH ISLA
19
CHARLESTOWN OF ABERLOUR
DUFFTOWN
HUNTLY
2
STRATHBOGIE
The Bin
The Bin Forest
ABERCHIRDER
BEN RINNES
Glen Rinnes
Glen Fiddich
Glenfiddich Forest
The Scalp
Glens of Foudland
Hill of Foudland
Knockandy Hill
Glenlivet
Corryhabbie Hill
Blackwater Forest
Mount of Haddoch
Rhynie
11
22
24
Correen Hills
Auchleven
Lumsden
The Buck
Hill of Three Stones
Ladder Hills
Lord Arthur's Hill
HOWE OF ALFORD
Alford
26
Cock Bridge
Delnadamph Lodge
Craig of Bunzeach
Pressendye
Mona Gowan
Tarland
Pitfichie Forest
Corrennie Forest
Benaquhallie
Speyside Way
A95
A96
A98
A97
A941
A920
A944
A939

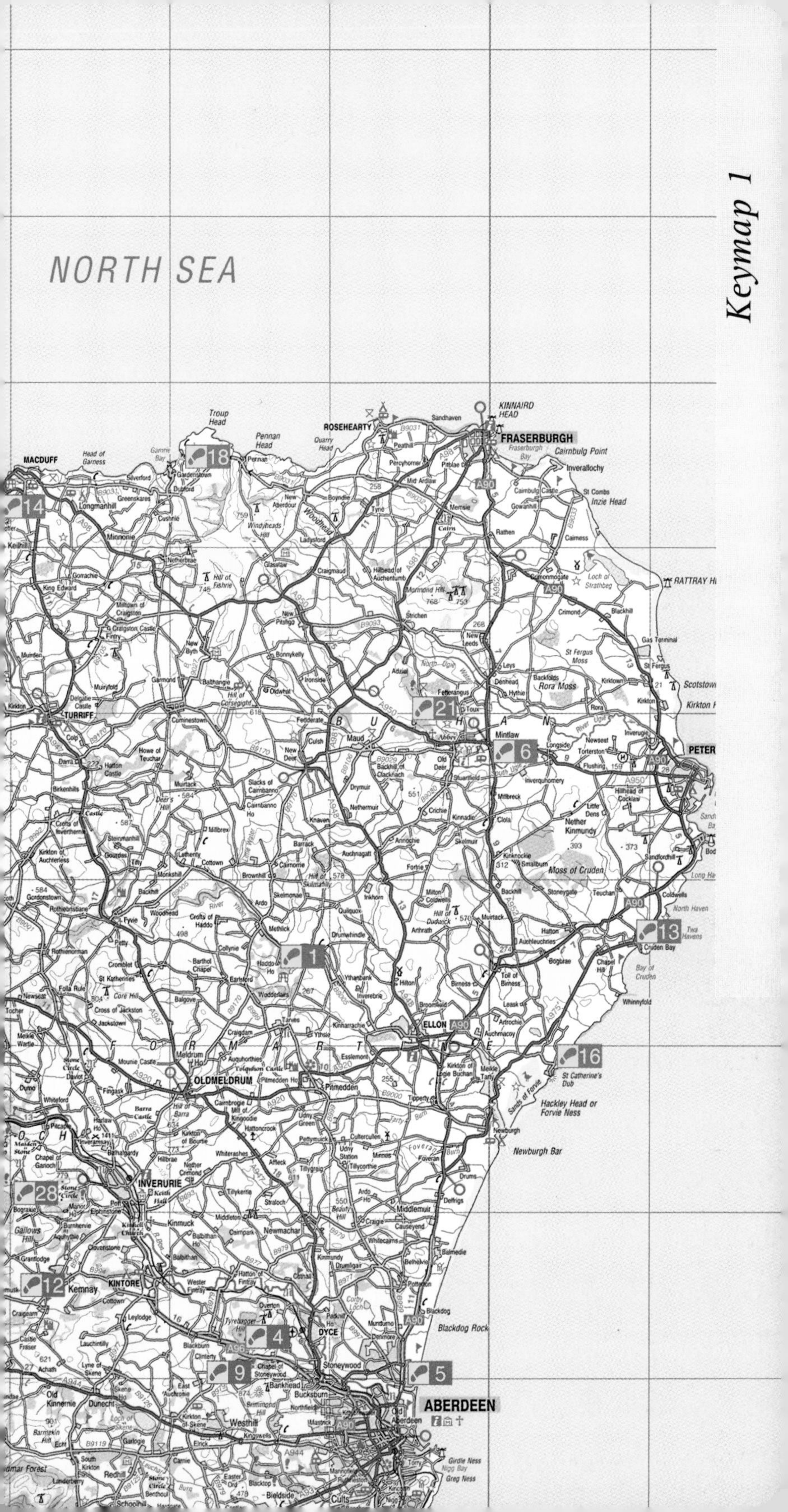
NORTH SEA
MACDUFF
Troup Head
Pennan Head
ROSEHEARTY
KINNAIRD HEAD
FRASERBURGH
Cairnbulg Point
Inverallochy
St Combs
Inzie Head
Sandhaven
Gardenstown
Pennan
New Aberdour
Longmanhill
Minnonie
King Edward
New Pitsligo
Strichen
Mormond Hill
New Byth
Crimonmogate
Loch of Strathbeg
RATTRAY H
Crimond
Gas Terminal
St Fergus
Scotstown
Kirkton H
PETER
TURRIFF
Cuminestown
Maud
New Deer
Fetterangus
B U C H A N
Mintlaw
Longside
Old Deer
Rora Moss
St Fergus Moss
Fyvie
Methlick
Haddo Ho
Ellon
Nether Kinmundy
Moss of Cruden
Hatton
Cruden Bay
Bay of Cruden
Whinnyfold
North Haven
Long Haven
F O R M A R T I N E
OLDMELDRUM
Tarves
Pitmedden
Udny Green
Newburgh
Sands of Forvie
Hackley Head or Forvie Ness
St Catherine's Dub
Newburgh Bar
INVERURIE
Kemnay
KINTORE
Newmachar
Balmedie
DYCE
Blackdog
Blackdog Rock
Stoneywood
Bucksburn
ABERDEEN
Westhill
Dunecht
Cults
Bieldside
Girdle Ness
Nigg Bay
Greg Ness
18
14
21
6
13
1
16
28
12
4
9
5

Keymap 2

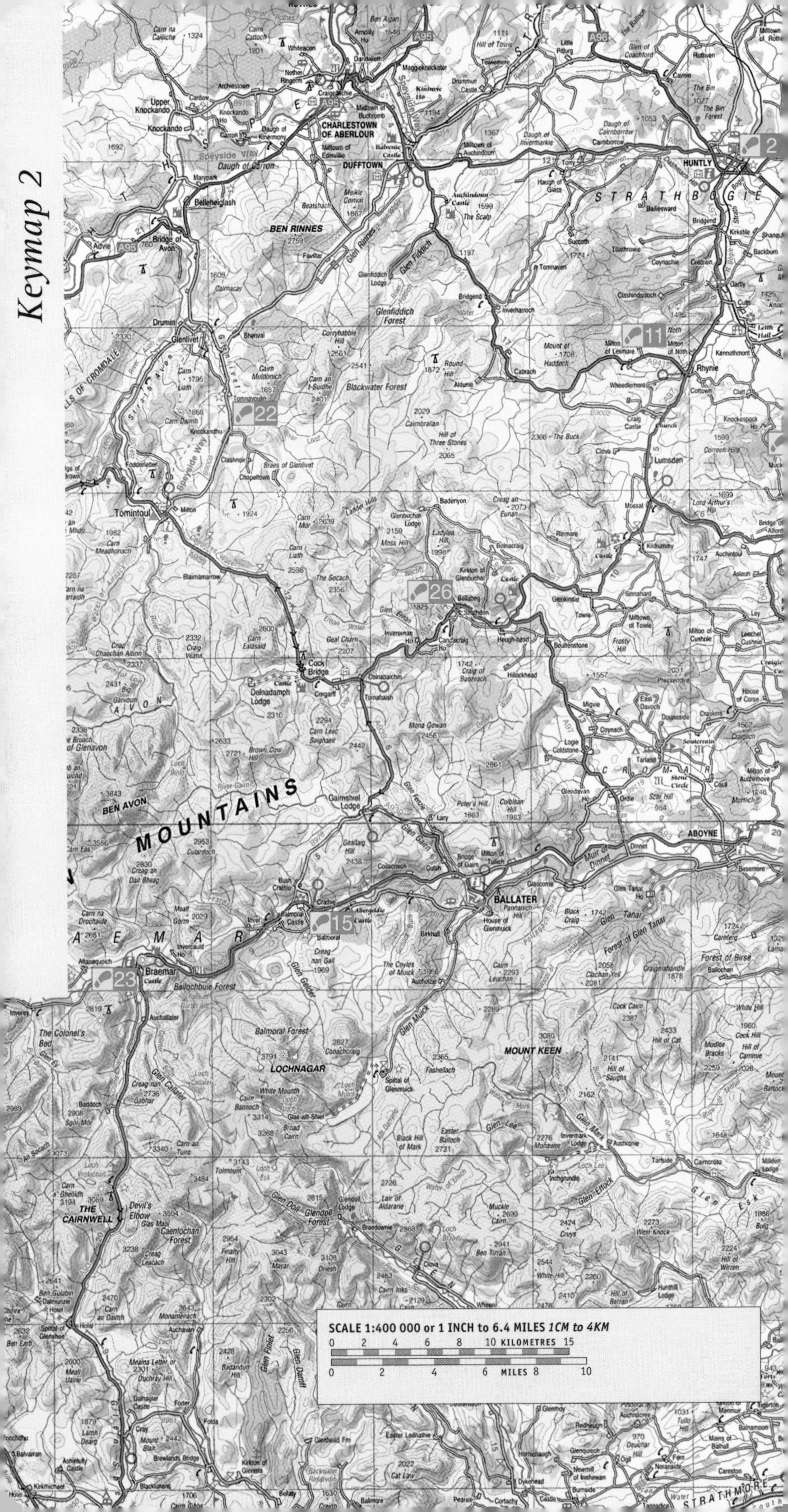

SCALE 1:400 000 or 1 INCH to 6.4 MILES 1CM to 4KM
0 2 4 6 8 10 KILOMETRES 15
0 2 4 6 MILES 8 10
CHARLESTOWN OF ABERLOUR
DUFFTOWN
HUNTLY
STRATHBOGIE
BEN RINNES
Glenfiddich Forest
Blackwater Forest
Tomintoul
Glenlivet
Speyside Way
Rhynie
Lumsden
Cock Bridge
Corgarff
Delnadamph Lodge
Strathdon
Gairnshiel Lodge
BEN AVON
MOUNTAINS
BALLATER
ABOYNE
CROMAR
Tarland
Balmoral Castle
Braemar
Ballochbuie Forest
Balmoral Forest
LOCHNAGAR
MOUNT KEEN
Glen Muick
Glen Tanar
Forest of Glen Tanar
Glen Clova
Glen Esk
Glen Doll
THE CAIRNWELL
Devil's Elbow
Caenlochan Forest
Spittal of Glenshee
Spittal of Glenmuick
STRATHMORE
2
11
15
22
23
26

Keymap 2

Walk	Page	Start	Nat. Grid Reference	Distance	Time	Highest point
Above Balmoral	47	Car park at Crathie church	NO264949	5½ miles (8.9km)	2½ hrs	1410ft (430m)
Aden Country Park and Deer Abbey	25	Car park of A952 north of Mintlaw	NJ999485	5½ miles (8.9km)	2½ hrs	147ft (45m)
Banchory, River Dee and Crathes Castle	76	Car park off Dee Street, Banchory	NO697955	8½ miles (13.7km)	4 hrs	246ft (75m)
The Bochel and Crombie Water	69	Tombae Quarry	NJ218257	6½ miles (10.5km)	3½ hrs	1181ft (360m)
Bunzeach Forest	80	Car park at Bellabeg	NJ353130	11½ miles (18.3km)	5 hrs	1476ft (450m)
Clachnaben	84	Off B974 north of Bridge of Dye	NO649869	6 miles (9.7km)	3½ hrs	1932ft (589m)
Collieston and the Sands of Forvie	50	Car park on north side of Collieston	NK042287	6 miles (9.7km)	3 hrs	144ft (44m)
Creag Choinnich and the Lion's Face	72	Car park at Braemar	NO152914	4½ miles (7.2km)	2½ hrs	1765ft (538m)
Crovie and Troup Head	56	Car park at Crovie	NJ807652	6½ miles (10.5km)	3½ hrs	367ft (112m)
Cruden Bay and the Bullers of Buchan	42	Cruden Bay	NK093363	5 miles (8km)	2½ hrs	108ft (33m)
Cullen and Portknockie	28	Cullen	NJ513671	4½ miles (7.2km)	2½ hrs	180ft (55m)
Deveron Valley	59	Milltown of Rothiemay	NJ548482	7 miles (11.3km)	3½ hrs	830ft (253m)
Duff House and the Bridge of Alvah	44	Duff House	NJ691633	5½ miles (8.9km)	2½ hrs	278ft (85m)
Elgin, River Lossie and Quarry Wood	62	Elgin cathedral	NJ222631	7 miles (11.3km)	3½ hrs	360ft (110m)
Elrick and Brimmond Hills	33	Kirkhill Forest	NJ847110	4½ miles (7.2km)	2 hrs	809ft (265m)
Forest of Deer	65	Car park at Drinnie's Wood	NJ974505	7 miles (11.3km)	3½ hrs	459ft (140m)
Haddo House and Country Park	14	Haddo Country Park	NJ867346	3 miles (4.8km)	1½ hrs	206ft (63m)
Huntly	16	Huntly	NJ529399	3 miles (4.8km)	1½ hrs	393ft (102m)
Inverbervie, Benholm and Gourdon	53	Inverbervie	NO832727	6½ miles (10.5km)	3 hrs	446ft (136m)
Kemnay and the River Don	40	Kemnay	NJ732162	5½ miles (8.9km)	2½ hrs	288ft (88m)
Laurencekirk and Denlethen Wood	18	Laurencekirk	NO719716	4 miles (6.4km)	2 hrs	229ft (70m)
Mither Tap, Oxen Craig and Craigshannoch	86	Bennachie Centre	NJ699216	9 miles (14.5km)	5½ hrs	1733ft (529m)
River Don, Beach and Old Aberdeen	22	Bridge of Don	NJ949095	5½ miles (8.9km)	2½hrs	147ft (45m)
Scolty Hill	36	Scolty Woodland Park	NO687947	3 miles (4.8km)	2 hrs	983ft (299m)
Stonehaven and Dunnottar Castle	30	Stonehaven	NO875858	4½ miles (7.2km)	2½ hrs	265ft (81m)
Suie Hill and Knock Saul	74	Car park at Suie	NJ546233	5½ miles (8.9km)	3hrs	1361ft (415m)
Tap o'Noth	38	Tap o'Noth Car Park	NJ481284	3 miles (4.8km)	2 hrs	1851ft (360m)
Tyrebagger Hill	20	Car park at Kirkhill Forest	NJ854116	4 miles (6.4km)	2 hrs	821ft (250m)

Comments

The walk starts at Crathie church, takes you past the graveyard in which John Brown is buried and continues up into the hills behind Balmoral Castle.
A flat walk, partly along a disused railway track and partly through the well-wooded grounds of Aden Country Park, leads to ruins of a medieval abbey.
This splendid walk follows the track of a disused railway beside the River Dee between Banchory and Crathes Castle and includes a short circuit of the wooded castle grounds.
This is one of the excellet series of well waymarked routes on the Glenlivet Estate. Much of it is around the valley of Crombie Water and there are extensive views.
A long but easy route to follow, mainly on clear and broad forest tracks, amidst the lonely grandeur of Strathdon.
An initial opening stretch through woodland is followed by a long, steady – though not particularly steep – ascent to the distinctive summit of Clachnaben.
There are superb views looking along the coast towards Aberdeen on this walk, most of which is across the Forvie National Nature Reserve.
After a short, steep climb to a spectacular viewpoint overlooking Braemar and the Cairngorms, the rest of the walk is a circuit of the wooded base of the hill.
A sharp descent into the tiny village of Crovie, huddled at the base of steep cliffs, is followed by a walk over Troup Head. The views along the Moray Firth are spectacular.
A walk along the rugged cliffs, passing the dramatic remains of an early 19th-century castle, leads to the impressive rock arch of the Bullers of Buchan.
This bracing coastal walk uses the track of a disused railway, passes the prominent Bow Fiddle Rock and takes you across the sands of Cullen Bay.
Both on the higher level opening stretch and on the low level return, there are fine views over the Deveron Valley.
An 18th-century Adam mansion, woodland and fine views of a gorge are the main ingredients of this interesting walk just inland from Banff.
From the grand ruins of Elgin Cathedral, the walk takes you through parkland beside the River Lossie for a short circuit of Quarry Wood.
Fairly easy climbs lead to two fine and extensive viewpoints near Aberdeen and the final stretch is through attractive woodland.
Much of this walk is through woodland and there are extensive views, especially from the Observatory near the end.
A splendid and elegant 18th-century mansion is the focal point for this short and easy walk around the former estate of the earls of Aberdeen.
From below the walls of Huntly Castle, you enjoy an attractive stroll beside the River Deveron before returning to the town.
After an inland first half along an old coach road, the return leg hugs the coast, passing through the fishing village of Gourdon.
This walk, the first half of which is through the grounds of the Fetternear Estate, explores a particularly attractive stretch of the Don valley.
There are extensive views over the flat and fertile country of The Howe of the Mearns and some attractive woodland on this walk.
There is attractive woodland at the beginning and end of this walk. In between – following a climb – you enjoy superb moorland walking and magnificent panoramic views.
The walk takes you through historic Old Aberdeen but also includes the Don estuary, a bracing stroll beside Aberdeen's beach and an attractive riverside park.
After walking through woodland around the base of the hill, a short but fairly steep climb brings you to a superb viewpoint over Deeside.
The outward leg is along the coast; the return is mainly through woodland. Highlights of the walk are the dramatic views of Dunnottar Castle.
This undulating walk along a section of the well waymarked Gordon Way is a mixture of moorland and woodland with several fine views .
A short climb to the summit of Tap o'Noth, site of an Iron Age fort, rewards you with a magnificent view over the surrounding countryside.
A winding but easy and gradual climb through woodland brings you to a fine viewpoint, crowned by an observation tower.

Introduction to Aberdeen and Royal Deeside

The slogan that the Aberdeen and Grampian Tourist Board uses to describe this region is 'Royal Deeside, Whisky, Castles and Coast' and no visitor can fail to be aware of these features. The royal connection is obviously most evident around Balmoral, both castles and distilleries litter the area – the latter particularly numerous around Speyside – and the long coastline stetches almost from Inverness to Montrose.

The area covered by this walking guide is that part of north-east Scotland that lies between the Cairngorms and the sea. It has in fact two coastlines, the North Sea and Moray Firth, and two major river valleys, the Dee and the Don. To the west it is bounded by the eastern edge of the Cairngorms and the valley of the Spey, although there is one walk included which is just to the west of that river. To the north and east it has the sea for its borders. Only to the south, where the fertile lowlands of the Howe of the Mearns merge almost imperceptibly into those further south, does the region lack a clearly defined natural frontier.

As the Cairngorms are covered in another Pathfinder title, there are no mountain walks in this guide. But this area is surrounded by mountains and there are plenty of hill-walking opportunities as the Grampian Highlands stretch eastwards towards the coast, reaching almost to the outskirts of Aberdeen.

It is a region that contains a great variety of attractive landscapes. Both coasts are dramatic and rugged, with cliffs and bold headlands broken up by estuaries, coves and broad sandy bays. On these estuaries a string of important ports and fishing harbours grew up – Stonehaven, Aberdeen, Peterhead, Fraserburgh, Macduff, Banff and Buckie – as well as many smaller ones.

Haddo Country Park

Aberdeen, the 'Granite City' and metropolis of the region, is Scotland's third largest city. It lies at the mouth of the River Dee and its rise was based on being a major port and the main centre of the

The harbour at Portknockie

Scottish fishing industry. In recent years it has become Britain's leading offshore oil centre. About $1^1/_2$ miles (2.4km) to the north of the city centre is Old Aberdeen near the mouth of the River Don. Old Aberdeen grew up around St Machar's Cathedral and King's College, one of the two constituent colleges of the University of Aberdeen, and its cobbled streets, dignified houses, college buildings and partly ruined cathedral enable it to still retain the air of a separate scholastic and ecclesiastical centre.

On either side of the city the Dee and Don empty into the North Sea, having flowed through beautiful and unspoilt valleys from their sources in the Cairngorms. In their upper reaches their valleys are narrow and enclosed by high hills but they later broaden out as they approach the coast.

Along the banks of the Dee are a succession of attractive towns, many of which have now become popular resorts – Banchory, Aboyne, Ballater and Braemar. Visitors are attracted to the area not only for its fine scenery, historic sites and good walking but also for its royal connections. These began in 1852 when Prince Albert purchased the Balmoral Estate. Three years later the castle was completed and since the reign of Queen Victoria, it has been a favourite royal residence.

The almost parallel valley of the Don is quieter and lonelier, austere in places, but undeniably attractive. Near the banks of the river are the villages and small towns of Inverurie, Kemnay, Alford, Bellabeg and Cock Bridge. Another attractive river is the Deveron which winds northwards towards the Moray Firth, passing below the walls of Huntly Castle and flowing into the sea between Banff and Macduff.

Eastwards from the main bulk of the Cairngorms stretch the Grampian Highlands, reaching almost to the North Sea coast and enclosing the valleys of the Dee, Don and other rivers. They provide fine hill walking – spectacular without being too strenuous or hazardous – and the hills are punctuated by a series of well-known and distinctive landmarks. These include Bennachie, Tap o'Noth, Scolty Hill and Clachnaben, all of which are featured in the selection of walks. Although lacking the height or severity of the adjacent Cairngorms, these hills must still be treated with respect and caution, especially in winter or in misty weather. Only experienced and properly equipped walkers, able to navigate by using a compass, should venture out onto them in such conditions.

The many forests throughout the area add an extra dimension to the variety of walking terrain. Here walkers can choose from a wide selection of trails of differing lengths and difficulties, well-waymarked by the Forestry Commission.

Fringing the coast are the lowlands where some of the finest and most productive agricultural land in Scotland is to be found. In the south are the rich pastures of the Howe of the Mearns. Further north is Buchan, the 'Land at the Bend in the Ocean' as the tourist literature likes to call it, a land of rolling plains, small coastal settlements and superb cliff scenery. Further west the lowlands extend along the Moray Firth towards Inverness.

This part of north-east Scotland is particularly rich in historic remains. Earliest of these are the numerous prehistoric stone circles and hillforts. The latter are associated with the mysterious Picts, whose heartland was in this area, and some of them – Tap o'Noth and Mither Tap – are featured in the walks.

Castles – medieval and later ones – are everywhere and the choice is almost overwhelming. Everyone has their favourites but few would disagree that the most dramatic of these is Dunnottar, perched precariously on the cliffs just to the south of Stonehaven. Other fine castles are Kildrummy, Glenbuchart, Crathes, Craigievar and Braemar, as well as Queen Victoria's Balmoral and the ruined 19th-century Slains Castle, the latter in almost as dramatic a location as Dunnottar.

Medieval church architecture is represented by the sparse remains of Deer Abbey near Mintlaw and the cathedrals at Aberdeen and Elgin. The final abolition of bishops in the Church of Scotland in the 17th century made cathedrals redundant and nowadays Aberdeen only comprises a nave and Elgin, the former seat of the bishops of Moray, is a ruin, but a particularly striking and beautiful one.

As the area became more settled and peaceful, especially after the union with England and the ending of the Jacobite rebellions, agriculture prospered and, in the late 18th and early 19th centuries, a number of towns and villages were redeveloped and rebuilt by their landowners. Laurencekirk, Huntly and Cullen are three examples of these. At the same time a number of large country houses were built. Most splendid of these is Haddo House, the former seat of the earls of Aberdeen, and Duff House, the

The view from Brimmond Hill

former home of the earls of Fife, both elegant Georgian mansions designed by the renowned Scottish architect William Adam.

All the 28 routes in this guide – including those on the hills – are relatively easy to follow and are almost entirely on clear paths and tracks. As well as hill walks, they embrace forest trails, coast and riverside paths and walks across parkland and through woodland. They also include stretches of disused railway tracks which provide well-surfaced routes for both cyclists and walkers.

The scenic variety, a wealth of historic attractions and generally clear and well-waymarked paths combine to make this an excellent walking area. A extra bonus is that the climate here is drier and sunnier, though not always warmer, than in the west of Scotland – one of the main reasons behind Prince Albert's choice of Balmoral. The Moray Firth coast has some of the driest weather and best sunshine records of anywhere in Britain.

The following selection of walks are spread over the whole of the area, embrace all the differing terrain and include many of the towns, villages and places of historic interest – Iron Age hillforts, castles, the cathedrals at Aberdeen and Elgin and country houses.

One final point but a most important one. From August onwards, when grouse-shooting and deer-stalking take place on the hills and moors, some of the walks may be restricted or closed at times. During this period you need to check with the local tourist information centre – details given on page 94–95 – or the relevant estate office.

Haddo House and Country Park

Start	Haddo Country Park, signposted from B9170 and B9005 to the south of Methlick
Distance	3 miles (4.8km)
Approximate time	1½ hours
Parking	Haddo Country Park
Refreshments	Tearoom at Haddo House
Ordnance Survey maps	Landranger 30 (Fraserburgh & Peterhead Pathfinder 199, NJ83/93 (Methlick & Ellon)

The grounds of Haddo House, now a country park, make a fine venue for a short, attractive and varied walk and there are several waymarked trails. This route combines two of them and includes parkland, woodland and a circuit of a lake, as well as the opportunity to visit a magnificent 18th-century house, now maintained by the National Trust for Scotland.

The elegant Georgian mansion of Haddo House was designed by the renowned Scottish architect William Adam and built in the 1730s. It was the residence of the earls of Aberdeen, one of whom – the 4th earl – was Prime Minister at the outbreak of the Crimean War in 1855. The house was refurbished in the late 19th century and since 1978 the house has been in the care of the National Trust for Scotland. It houses a fine art collection.

Haddo House

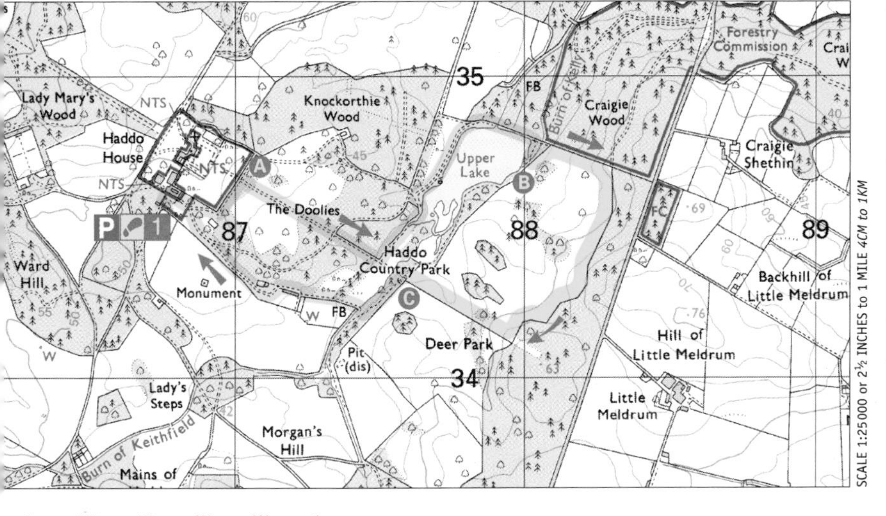

0 200 400 600 800 METRES 1 KILOMETRES MILES
0 200 400 600 YARDS ½

From the car park take the path signed to Haddo House and in front of the stable block, turn right, in the 'Country Park, Lake, Walks and Woodland' direction. After passing through a gate, bear left off the tarmac track onto a path which curves left and in front of gates to the house, turn right along a straight path, known as the Scots Mile Ⓐ.

Just before reaching a duck pond on the right, turn left, at a blue-waymarked post, along a path which enters trees and continues along the wooded shores of the lake. At a T-junction, turn right to continue beside the lake and at the next T-junction, turn right again. Cross a bridge over an outlet burn, walk across the end of the lake and the path curves right to cross another footbridge over the Burn of Kelly.

Immediately turn sharp left Ⓑ – almost doubling back – to walk along a broad grassy path which bends right and continues alongside a wall on the left. The path bends right again, now by woodland on the left, and winds across the park to a T-junction. To the left are two statues of deer and beyond them a large urn. The latter was placed here by the 4th earl as a memorial to his first wife. Turn right along the tree-lined Scots Mile again and after going through the ornamental Golden Gates, turn left Ⓒ, at a blue-waymarked post, along a path through trees.

The path turns right, crosses a footbridge over a burn and at the fork immediately ahead, take the left-hand path. Following the regular blue waymarks, keep ahead across a field to a well in the far left corner, turn right along the field edge and at the next waymarked post, turn left through a line of trees. Turn right again along the left edge of the trees and turn left up steps to pass in front of the Pheasantry. Despite its name, it is unlikely that this brick building, erected in 1885, ever housed pheasants. It was originally used as a hen house, later converted into cottages for estate workers and is now a Field Studies Centre.

Bear left along a tarmac track which curves right and leads back to the start. On the way you pass a giant beech tree, the largest at Haddo and reputed to be the largest in north east Scotland with an exceptional spread of around 115ft (35m). There is also an obelisk seen on the left, a monument to the 4th earl's brother who was killed at the Battle of Waterloo. ●

Huntly

Start	Huntly
Distance	3 miles (4.8km)
Approximate time	1½ hours
Parking	Huntly
Refreshments	Pubs and cafés at Huntly
Ordnance Survey maps	Landranger 29 (Banff), Pathfinders 181NJ44/54 (Huntly [North]) and 197, NJ43 (Huntly [South])

After an opening stretch along a tree-lined avenue to the imposing ruins of Huntly Castle and a view of the dramatic Deveron Gorge, much of this short walk follows an attractive riverside path beside the Deveron. On the return leg, you pass through some fine woodland on the edge of the town.

The old town of Huntly was redesigned on a grid-iron plan in the 18th century by the dukes of Gordon who lived in the nearby castle. Start in The Square, walk along Castle Street, passing the war memorial, and keep ahead along a tree-

Huntly Castle

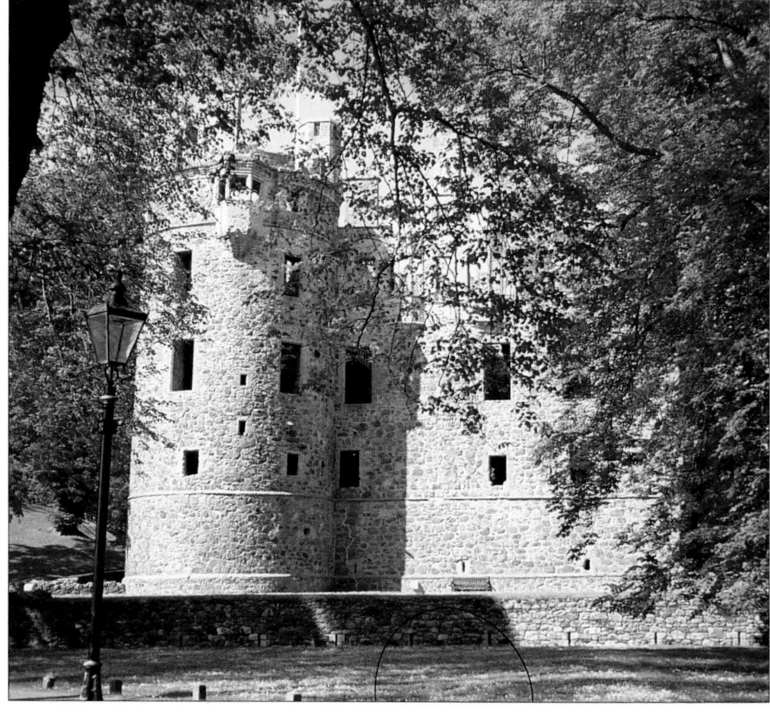

lined avenue. Go under the arch of Gordon School and continue down the avenue to the ruins of Huntly Castle. This impressive pile, finely situated above the River Deveron, is largely a 16th-century rebuilding of an earlier castle, partly reconstructed in the early 17th century following damage. It fell into disuse after the Civil War and became ruined.

Keep along the road which curves right, following the base of the castle mound, and you then turn sharp left along a track Ⓐ, almost doubling back. A brief detour ahead brings you to Castle Bridge from where there is a dramatic view of the Deveron Gorge.

After turning left along the track, cross a bridge, turn right through a car park and continue along a well-surfaced path beside the River Deveron. There are attractive views downstream on this stretch of the route. Pass under the first bridge, Ⓑ using a boardwalk, and keep along the riverside path to the next bridge. Further on the path becomes uneven, badly overgrown and difficult and at this point it is best to retrace your steps to the first bridge and climb the steps in front of it up to the road.

Turn right and just before reaching cemetery gates, bear left Ⓒ along a wooded path, by the cemetery wall on the right, later continuing through trees parallel to a road. Cross Riverside Drive and take the path ahead through more woodland and by garden walls to emerge onto a road. Turn right and then turn left Ⓓ along Deveron Street which leads back to The Square. ●

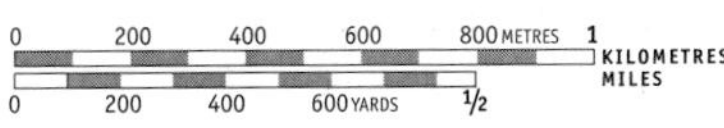

SCALE 1:25 000 or 2½ INCHES to 1 MILE 4CM to 1KM

Laurencekirk and Denlethen Wood

Start	Laurencekirk
Distance	4 miles (6.4km)
Approximate time	2 hours
Parking	Laurencekirk
Refreshments	Pubs and cafés at Laurencekirk
Ordnance Survey maps	Landranger 45 (Stonehaven & Banchory Pathfinder 285, NO67/77 (Laurencekirk & Fettercairn)

On this short and easy walk, there are a series of extensive views across the gently undulating and fertile farming country of the Howe of the Mearns to the hills of the Mounth. At the approximate half-way point, the route passes through Denlethen Wood, an attractive mixture of mainly pine, larch and spruce.

Laurencekirk is a planned village, laid out in the 1770s by Francis Lord Gardenstone, and it has become the main agricultural centre of the wide fertile plain of the Howe of the Mearns. The walk starts by the church at the north end of the long main street, at the corner of Kirkburn and High Street.

Walk along High Street through the

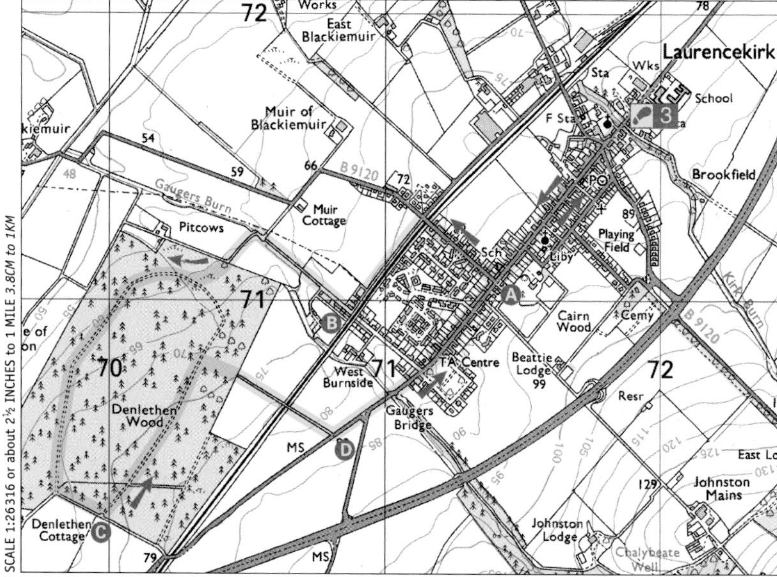

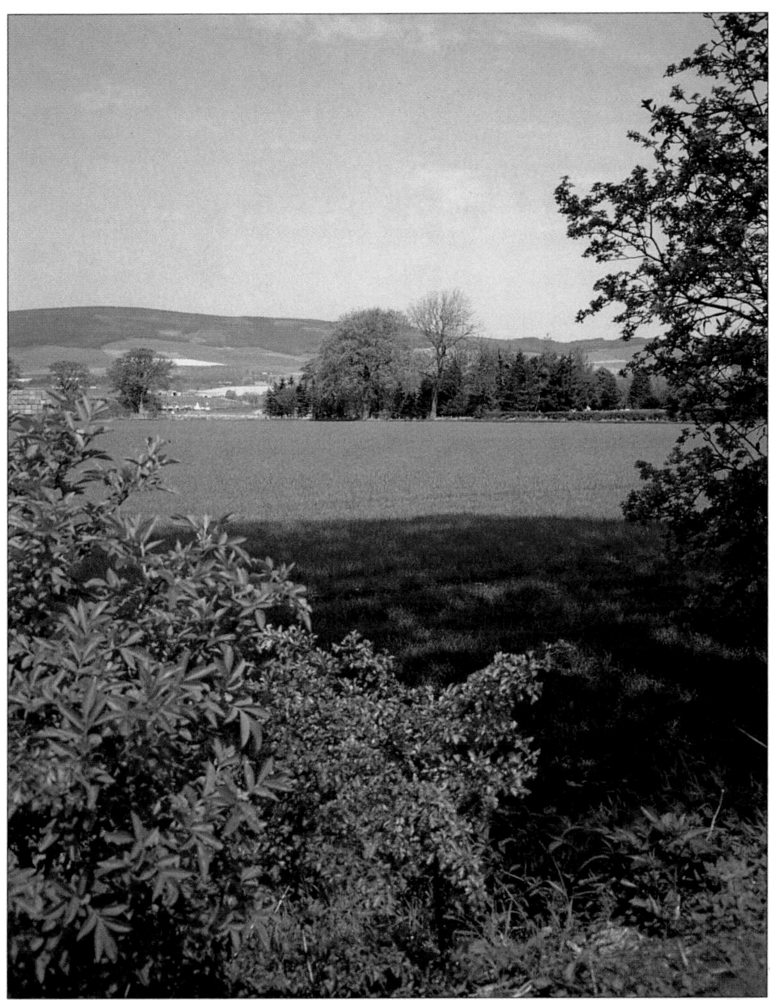

Howe of the Mearns near Laurencekirk

village and after ½ mile (800m), turn right Ⓐ along the B9120, signposted to Fettercairn. Immediately after crossing a railway bridge, turn left along a tarmac drive parallel to the railway line, follow the drive to the right Ⓑ and where it turns left, keep ahead along a straight, fence-lined path. On joining a track, continue along it, turning left to cross Gaugers Burn, and where the track bends right, keep ahead along a path to enter Denlethen Wood.

At a T-junction, turn right along a track which curves gradually left to another T-junction. Turn left to continue along the right edge of the wood and take the first track on the left to re-enter it Ⓒ. When you see a path on the right, turn onto it and go through a gate on the edge of the wood. Keep ahead along an enclosed track, cross a railway bridge and continue to a lane Ⓓ. Ahead is a view of the Hill of Garvock, crowned by a tower.

Turn left along the lane and where it bends right to a T-junction, keep ahead across grass and then continue along the road into Laurencekirk. Walk through the village to return to the start.

Tyrebagger Hill

Start	Kirkhill Forest car park, signposted from A96 near Dyce Airport
Distance	4 miles (6.4km)
Approximate time	2 hours
Parking	Kirkhill Forest
Refreshments	None
Ordnance Survey maps	Landranger 38 (Aberdeen, Inverurie & Pitmedden), Pathfinder 230, NJ81/91 (Dyce)

Like Elrick and Brimmond hills, which lie just to the south (Walk 9), Tyrebagger Hill is easily accessible from Aberdeen and lies within the confines of Kirkhill Forest. Both the ascent and descent through the forest are relatively undemanding and easy to follow and there are fine views from the tower on the 821-foot (250m) summit.

The view from Tyrebagger Hill

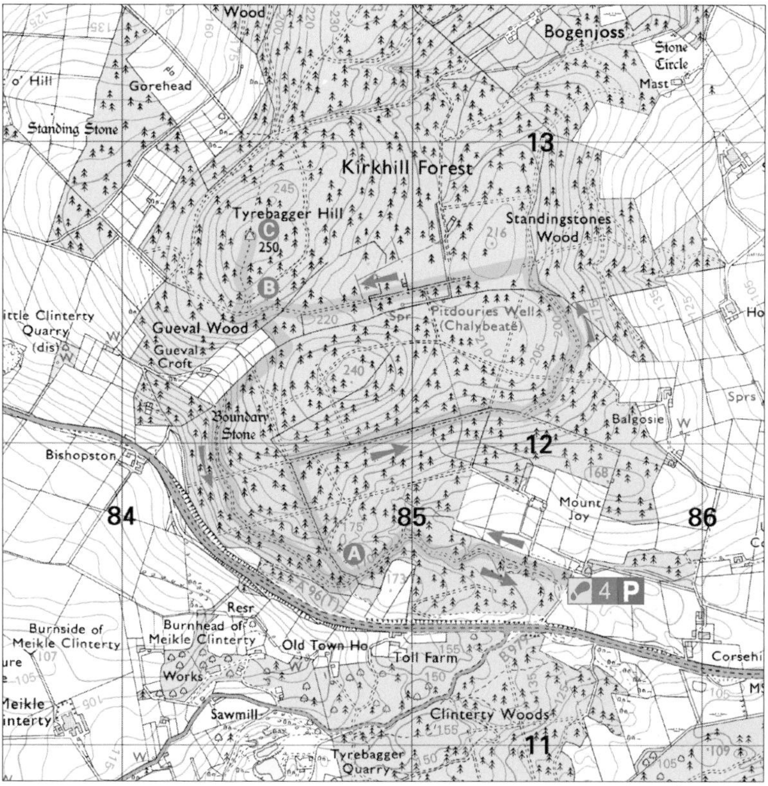

SCALE 1:25 000 or 2½ INCHES to 1 MILE 4CM to 1KM

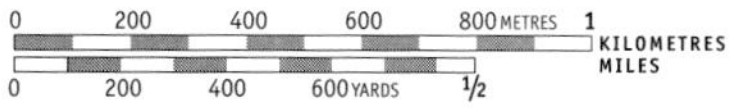

Start by heading across to the information board at the far end of the car park and keep ahead – passing beside a barrier – along the broad, straight, well-surfaced main track through the forest. The route is a white-waymarked one all the way but take care to only follow white footpath directions – those with a footprint symbol – as there are also white cycle trails and orienteering routes in Kirkhill Forest.

The track winds gently uphill and at a fork Ⓐ, take the right hand main track which curves right and continues uphill. Keep on this main track all the time – at one point it does a sharp right bend, later it bends left and then curves right again – to eventually reach a T-junction. Turn left along a straight track to a waymarked post Ⓑ, keep ahead along the track and at a footpath sign turn right onto a path that heads up through trees to the stone tower and triangulation pillar on the summit of Tyrebagger Hill, 821-ft (250m) high Ⓒ. From here there are particularly fine views looking westwards across Aberdeenshire.

Retrace your steps to the waymarked post Ⓑ and turn right along a path which heads downhill into woodland. The path curves left to keep along the right inside edge of the trees, bends right and continues downhill through an attractive area of mixed woodland. It then curves gradually left and finally ascends to reach the main forest track again Ⓐ.

Turn right, here rejoining the outward route, and retrace your steps to the start. ●

River Don, Beach and Old Aberdeen

Start	Bridge of Don, Donmouth Road car park
Distance	5½ miles (8.9km)
Approximate time	2½ hours
Parking	Donmouth Road
Refreshments	Pub at Bridge of Don, pub and café at Old Aberdeen, coffee shop at King's College Visitor Centre
Ordnance Survey maps	Landranger 38 (Aberdeen, Inverurie & Pitmedden), Pathfinder 246, NJ80/90 (Aberdeen)

There is plenty of variety on this walk on the north side of Aberdeen. It starts at a nature reserve by the estuary of the River Don, continues along a promenade beside Aberdeen's sandy beach and then heads across to the attractive university quarter of Old Aberdeen. The final leg is through parkland and beside the river again. Historic interest is provided by King's College and the cathedral in Old Aberdeen, and a picturesque medieval bridge over the Don.

Turn left out of the car park along Donmouth Road to the Bridge of Don, turn left to cross it and turn left Ⓐ alongside the river to its mouth. The stretch of the River Don between the Brig o'Balgownie and the sea forms the Donmouth Local Nature Reserve, an area of dunes, mudflats and the wooded banks of the river, noted for its birdlife.

Follow the road – the Esplanade – to the right, later descending to continue along a promenade above the beach and below the road embankment. After about 1 mile (1.6km), turn right under a tunnel Ⓑ and walk along a tarmac track to a road. Keep ahead to a road junction and turn right along Golf Road, passing between Kings Links Golf Centre and Course on the right and Pittodrie Stadium – home of Aberdeen Football Club – on the left. Turn left into Regent Walk Ⓒ, passing in front of three tower blocks, and at a crossroads turn left. Take the first road on the right (University Road) and at a T-junction, turn right Ⓓ along the attractive, cobbled High Street in Old Aberdeen. The buildings of King's College are to the right.

Old Aberdeen is based around King's College, the oldest part of Aberdeen University, and the cathedral and is located near the mouth of the River Don. The 'New Town' grew up around the mouth of the River Dee and has become the main focus of the present city, although Old Aberdeen still retains its separate and distinctive character. The chapel of King's College, noted for its splendid crown spire, dates from around 1500.

Where High Street divides in front of

0 200 400 600 800 METRES 1 KILOMETRES
0 200 400 600 YARDS ½ MILES

SCALE 1:25 000 or 2½ INCHES to 1 MILE *4CM to 1KM*

a handsome 18th-century building, formerly the town house, take the left fork. Cross a main road and keep ahead along The Chanonry, lined by fine 18th- and 19th-century granite houses, to St Machar's Cathedral. The present church, which dates mainly from the 15th and early 16th centuries, only comprises the nave and west front; the choir and transepts were destroyed when the central tower fell down in 1688. Nevertheless it is an interesting building with a superb, early 16th-century wooden ceiling in the nave. The west front, which has two short towers, is a striking if rather severe composition.

Beyond St Machar's Cathedral, bear right through a gate into Seaton Park and at the three-way fork immediately ahead **E**, take the left-hand path which heads downhill towards the river. At the next fork, continue along the right hand downhill path which curves right at the bottom and later keeps beside the wooded banks of the Don. Soon after joining the river another fork is reached and you take the right-hand uphill path through trees, following the river round a right bend. At this stage the Don flows through what is virtually a wooded gorge.

Leave the park by going through a

gate onto a road, turn left downhill and after a right bend, keep ahead to cross the medieval Brig o'Balgownie over the river. This attractive structure is one of the oldest bridges in Britain, built around 1320 allegedly at the behest of Robert the Bruce.

After crossing the bridge, turn right down steps and turn left to continue along a riverside path to the Bridge of Don. Keep ahead along Donmouth Road to return to the start.

King's College Chapel in Old Aberdeen

Aden Country Park and Deer Abbey

Start	Mintlaw, car park off A952 to the north of the village centre and just beyond where the disused railway track crosses the road
Distance	5½ miles (8.9km)
Approximate time	2½ hours
Parking	Mintlaw
Refreshments	Pubs and cafe at Mintlaw, cafe at Aden Country Park, pub at Old Deer
Ordnance Survey maps	Landranger 30 (Fraserburgh & Peterhead), Pathfinder 183, NJ84/94 (New Deer & Maud)

There is plenty of interest on this almost entirely flat walk in the Buchan countryside a few miles inland from Peterhead. The opening and closing stretches are along a disused railway track and in between you walk through the well-wooded grounds of a former estate, now Aden Country Park, passing the North East of Scotland Agricultural Heritage Centre and the remains of Aden House. The walk also includes a short detour to the medieval ruins of Deer Abbey.

The Formartine and Buchan Way is a footpath and cycle way created from part of the former Aberdeen-Peterhead-Fraserburgh railway. The railway was completed in 1865 and closed to passengers exactly 100 years later.

Begin by walking along the track, in the Maud direction, and after ½ mile (800m), you pass the ruined buildings of the former Mintlaw station. Continue along the track which eventually curves left to emerge onto a road **A**. Cross over and turn left onto a path that enters the woodlands of Aden Country Park. The path bends first right and then turns left to a T-junction. Turn right, in the direction of a green waymark, at the next T-junction turn right again alongside the lake, keep ahead and take the first path on the left. At a T-junction turn left again and at the next junction of paths, turn right and then right again to the North East of Scotland Agricultural Heritage Centre. This is

The ruins of Deer Abbey

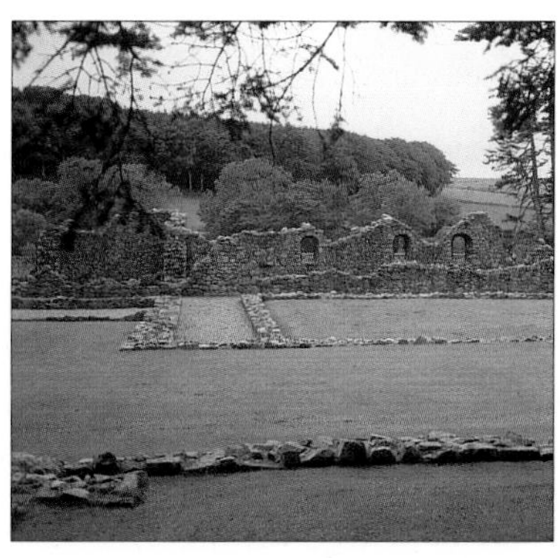

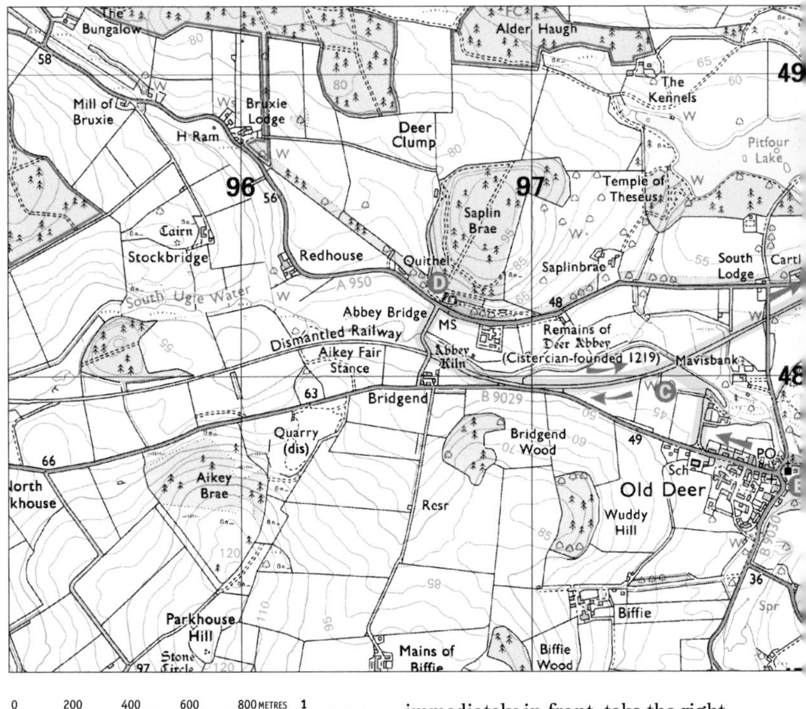

0 200 400 600 800 METRES 1 KILOMETRES

0 200 400 600 YARDS ½ MILES

housed in a unique and imposing semi-circular steading (or farmstead) and is well worth a visit.

Bear left to pass the former coach house and at a footpath sign to Mansion House and Old Deer, pass through a wall gap and walk along a path to the remains of Aden House. This was built in the late 18th century for the Russell family, the owners of the estate, and was reconstructed and enlarged in 1832. The Russells were responsible for the extensive planting of the trees and shrubs which transformed what had previously been a rather bare landscape. After the estate was sold in 1937, it was neglected until purchased by the local council in 1975 and subsequently restored and designated a country park.

Soon after passing the house, you re-enter trees and cross a bridge over South Ugie Water. At a fork immediately in front, take the right hand path which keeps by the wall bordering the churchyard of Old Deer church and goes through a gate onto a road in the village **B**. Walk along Abbey Street and at a sign 'Formartine and Buchan Way', turn right onto a track. At a fork take the left hand path which bends left alongside South Ugie Water and heads up to rejoin the disused railway track **C**. Turn left and follow it to a road – this is the short detour to Deer Abbey – turn right and at a T-junction **D**, turn right to the abbey. These atmospheric and tranquil remains are of a Cistercian abbey founded in 1219. The famous Book of Deer Abbey, a 9th-century manuscript now in the University Library at Cambridge, came from an earlier Celtic monastery.

Return to the Formartine and Buchan Way, turn left along it, in the Mintlaw direction, and follow it to a road **A**. Here you pick up the outward route and retrace your steps to the start. ●

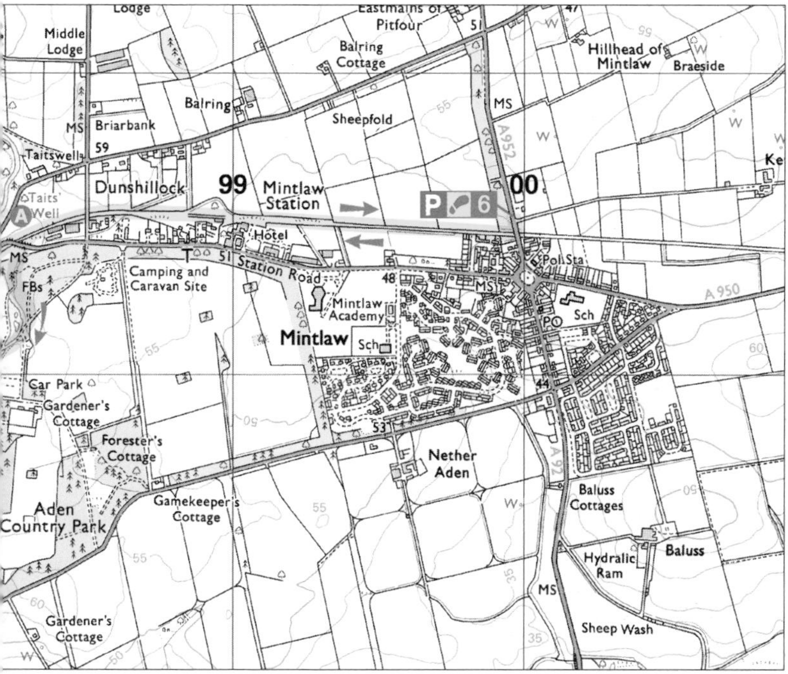

SCALE 1:25 000 or 2½ INCHES to 1 MILE *4CM to 1KM*

Aden Country Park

Cullen and Portknockie

Start	Cullen
Distance	4½ miles (7.2km)
Approximate time	2½ hours
Parking	Cullen, The Square
Refreshments	Pubs and cafés at Cullen, hotel at Cullen Bay, pubs at Portknockie
Ordnance Survey maps	Landranger 29 (Banff), Landrangers 147, NJ36/46 (Buckie) and 148, NJ56/66 (Banff & Cullen)

This enjoyable coastal walk uses roads and a disused railway track on the first half of the route between the fishing ports of Cullen and Portknockie. The return leg takes you along a spectacular cliff path, passing the impressive Bow Fiddle Rock, before descending to the broad, firm sands of Cullen Bay. After walking across the sands, the route continues on through Seatown and back to the start.

Cullen is a planned village, laid out in the early 1800s by the Earl of Seafield, and reached its height as a fishing port in the 1890s. It is famous for Cullen Skink, a soup made from smoked haddock, potatoes, milk and onions.

Begin in The Square and walk downhill towards the sea, passing under a disused railway viaduct. The railway was opened in 1886 and the impressive Cullen Viaducts were constructed because the Countess of Seafield did not want the line to go across the grounds of her house. Follow the road to the left, pass under another viaduct, cross a bridge over the Burn of Cullen and continue along the road as far as the imposing Cullen Bay Hotel.

Opposite the hotel – and just before the road bends left – turn right Ⓐ down steps to the disused railway track and turn left along it. Follow the track, initially between an embankment on the left and a golf course on the right and later through a cutting, to emerge onto a road in Portknockie Ⓑ. Cross the

Bow Fiddle Rock

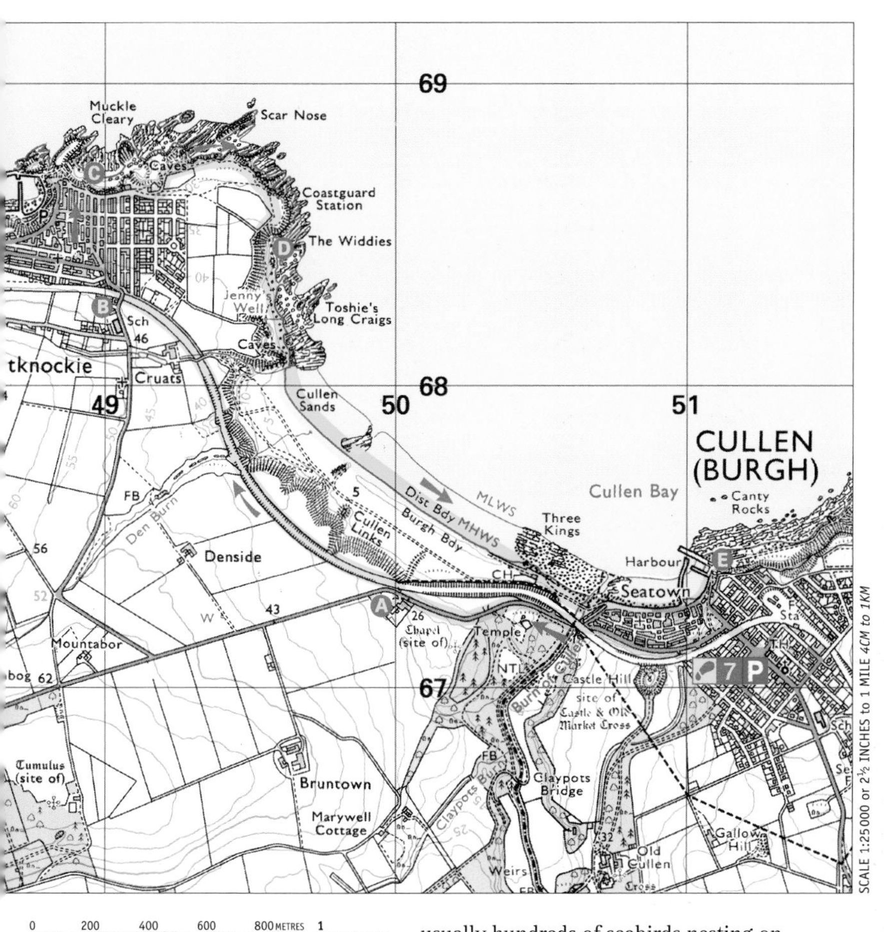

road, keep ahead down Bridge Street, pass to the left of a war memorial into Victoria Place and continue down towards the sea to a T-junction Ⓒ.

A short detour to the left brings you to a fine viewpoint above the harbour but the route continues to the right. At a junction of roads, keep ahead along the lower road, following signs to Bow Fiddle Rock, and where the road ends, turn left towards the sea to join a path. Take the right hand path at a fork which bears right and continues along the top of the cliffs, passing the impressive Bow Fiddle Rock. It gets its name from the natural archway in it caused by sea erosion and, from certain angles, this resembles the bow of a fiddle. There are usually hundreds of seabirds nesting on the rock.

Keep along the clifftop path which curves right and on joining a well-surfaced path at a fence corner, turn left Ⓓ and descend a long flight of steps, continuing along the shore and below cliffs to emerge onto the broad, firm sands of Cullen Bay. Walk across the sands and at the far end, climb steps onto a promenade. Continue along it to where it ends and keep ahead to cross a footbridge over the Burn of Cullen to the left of the viaduct.

Walk along the seafront through Seatown, virtually a separate settlement from Cullen. Its mainly 18th- and 19th-century cottages near the harbour are threaded by a maze of narrow lanes. On reaching a road Ⓔ, turn sharp right and head uphill to return to the start. ●

Stonehaven and Dunnottar Castle

Start	Stonehaven, Market Square
Distance	4½ miles (7.2km)
Approximate time	2½ hours
Parking	Market Square or Harbour at Stonehaven
Refreshments	Pubs and cafés at Stonehaven
Ordnance Survey maps	Landranger 45 (Stonehaven & Banchory), Pathfinder 273, NO87/88 (Stonehaven & Inverbervie)

Soon after ascending the cliffs above Stonehaven harbour comes the first glimpse of the dramatically sited ruins of Dunnottar Castle and the views become even more spectacular as you approach the castle along the clifftop path. In complete contrast, much of the return route is through the delightful Dunnottar Woods. Harbour, cliffs, coastal views, castle and woodland all combine to create a most exhilarating, satisfying and, at the same time, relatively undemanding walk.

The walk begins in the spacious Market Square in Stonehaven, an attractive fishing port and seaside resort. Facing the early 19th-century Market Buildings, pass to the right of them, cross a road and keep ahead along Market Lane to the beach.

Turn right along a path to the harbour, crossing a footbridge over Carron Water, and at the harbour, keep ahead through the car park and turn right along a road, passing the Tolbooth. This is the oldest building in Stonehaven and was originally built in the late 16th century as a storehouse for Dunnottar Castle. Later it became a courthouse and prison and now it is a museum and restaurant. Turn left along Shorehead, following the curve of the harbour, turn right **A** along Wallace Wynd and turn left into Castle Street. Where this narrow road ends, keep ahead along a steeply ascending path which bends left and continues up to emerge onto a road on the clifftop. From here there are grand views to the left over Stonehaven town and harbour.

Keep ahead and where the road bends sharply right, bear right **B** onto a gently ascending, fence-lined, tarmac path, passing to the left of a war memorial. A metal kissing gate on the right gives access to it, a magnificent viewpoint. Past the kissing gate the path become a rough, narrower one and soon you get the first views of Dunnottar Castle. The castle remains in sight for most of the next ¾ mile (1.2km).

Climb a stile, keep ahead around the curving rim of Strathlethan Bay to climb another one and walk across a field to cross a footbridge over a burn and climb another stile. Keep by the right field edge, climb a stile and continue along a winding and undulating path above the bay of Castle Haven to the castle.

Although in a seemingly impregnable position – situated on a great sandstone rock that rises almost vertically from the sea, lapped by the water on three sides and almost detached from the mainland – Dunnottar Castle has been captured on several occasions. The last of these was in 1652 when it surrendered to the forces of Oliver Cromwell. Dominating the ruins are the 14th-century L-shaped keep and the 16th-century gatehouse. The castle was dismantled after the 1715 Jacobite Rebellion.

By the steps that lead down to the castle, follow the path to the right, keep ahead along a track and pass through a gate beside a lodge onto a road. Turn right and take the first turning on the left C to continue along a narrow lane towards radio masts. The lane curves right and then heads gently downhill to

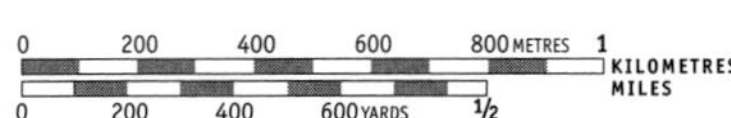

SCALE 1:25000 or 2½ INCHES to 1 MILE 4CM to 1KM

emerge onto a main road Ⓓ. Turn right, follow the road round a right bend and then turn sharp left along a lane signposted to Dunnottar Nurseries.

Just after crossing a bridge over the Burn of Glaslaw, turn right beside a barrier Ⓔ onto a path through Dunnottar Woods. At an immediate fork by a footpath sign, take the right hand lower path, signposted to Shell House, through the woods and above the burn, passing to the right of the Shell House, a small folly decorated with seashells. The path later bears left away from the burn and heads up to another footpath sign. On joining another path, bear right, in the Carron Gate direction, continue near the top left edge of the trees and at the next footpath sign, bear right downhill to emerge from the wood and pass beside a barrier onto a road.

Keep ahead to a T-junction, turn right along Low Wood Road and opposite a road on the right, turn left onto a tarmac path Ⓕ beside a strip of grass on the left. The path curves right beside Carron Water to a footbridge. Turn left over it, keep ahead along Ann Street and take the first turning on the right to return to the Market Square. ●

Dunnottar Castle

Elrick and Brimmond Hills

Start	Kirkhill Forest, Tyrebagger Sculptures car park, off B979 ½ mile (800m) south west of its junction with the A96
Distance	4½ miles (7.2km)
Approximate time	2 hours
Parking	Tyrebagger Sculptures car park
Refreshments	None
Ordnance Survey maps	Landranger 38 (Aberdeen, Inverurie & Pitmedden), Pathfinders 230, NJ81/91 (Dyce) and 246, NJ80/90 (Aberdeen)

The adjacent Elrick and Brimmond hills rise above the conifers of Kirkhill Forest and offer some of the best hill walking in the immediate vicinity of Aberdeen. Although of modest heights, the views from them are extensive and the paths are clear and well-waymarked. After descending from Brimmond Hill, the remainder of the route is through attractive woodland. Part of the walk follows a woodland Sculpture Trail.

With your back to the road, take the uphill track straight ahead into the forest, following a brown-waymarked route. At a fork, take the right-hand track which bends left downhill but look out for where you turn right off it to cross a succession of footbridges over small burns.

Keep ahead gently uphill, turning left by a picnic area, turning right to continue up between heather, gorse and trees, and then bending left alongside a wall on the right to a fork. Take the right-hand uphill path which continues over the open hillside to reach the cairn and picnic area at the top of Elrick Hill **A**. Although only 662ft (202m) high, this is a fine viewpoint and the radio masts on Brimmond Hill, the next objective, can be seen ahead.

Head downhill quite steeply into woodland again, descend a flight of steps to a car park and walk along a track to a lane **B**. Climb the steps opposite and head uphill to a stile. After climbing it, bear slightly right through an area of gorse and continue parallel to the bottom right-hand field edge – still following brown waymarks – to a Brimmond Hill information board. At this point, turn left and head steeply uphill across the grassy slopes, making for a footpath post seen on the horizon. Continue past it to the next post and on to climb a stile on the far side of the field **C**.

Turn right along the right field edge to join a tarmac track in front of another stile. Climb it, keep ahead along the track but shortly bear right onto a steadily ascending path. Take the left-hand path at a fork and continue up to the radio masts, picnic area and triangulation pillar on the summit of Brimmond Hill, 869ft (265m) high **D**. The contrasting views take in Aberdeen,

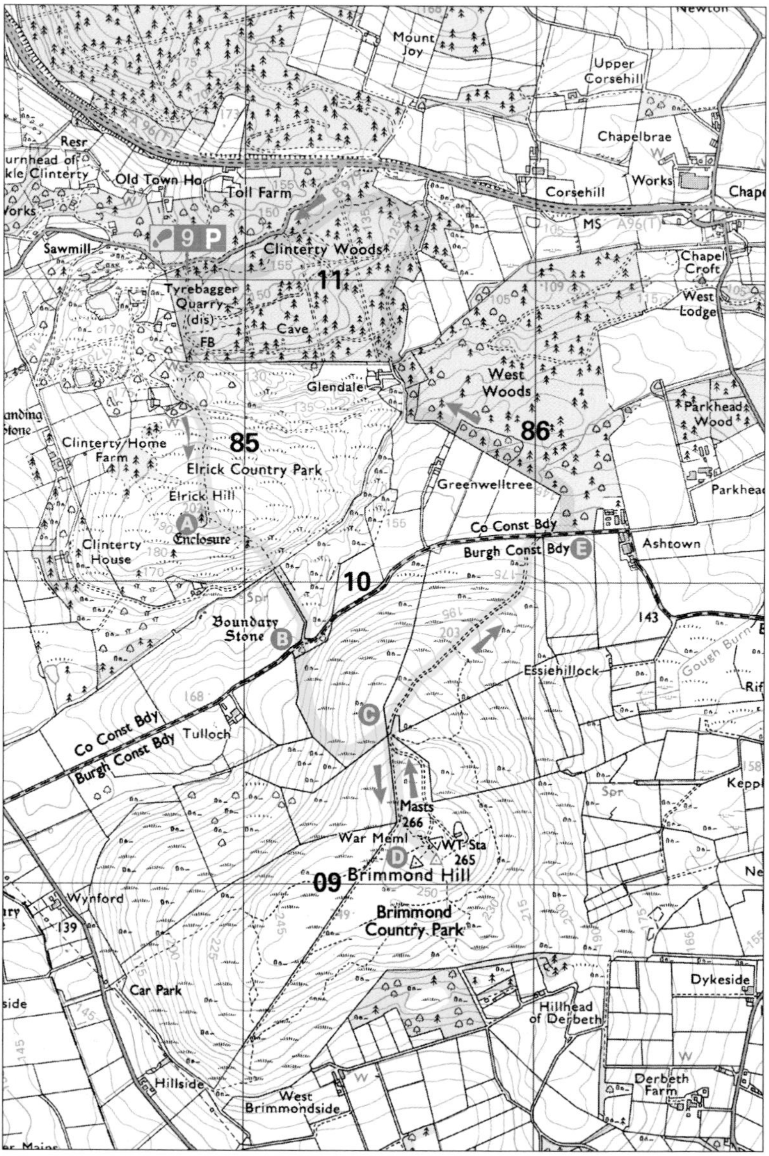

SCALE 1:25 000 or 2½ INCHES to 1 MILE *4CM to 1KM*

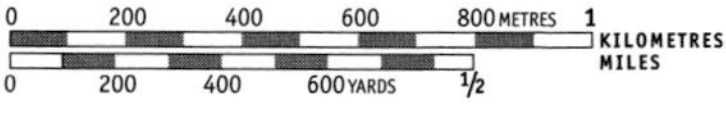

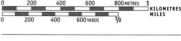

the coast, Elrick Hill and a large slice of rural Aberdeenshire, including – in clear conditions – the prominent landmarks of Bennachie and Clachnaben.

Retrace your steps to the last stile and continue along the tarmac track which descends to a metal kissing-gate. Go through, walk through a car park to a lane, turn right and at a brown-waymarked post and a 'Four Hills Walk West Woods' sign, turn left through another kissing gate Ⓔ. Take the downhill path along the left inside edge of woodland, cross a track, bear slightly left and continue along the left inside edge of the trees. Over to the left is a golf course. The path descends, bends right and at a brown-waymarked post,

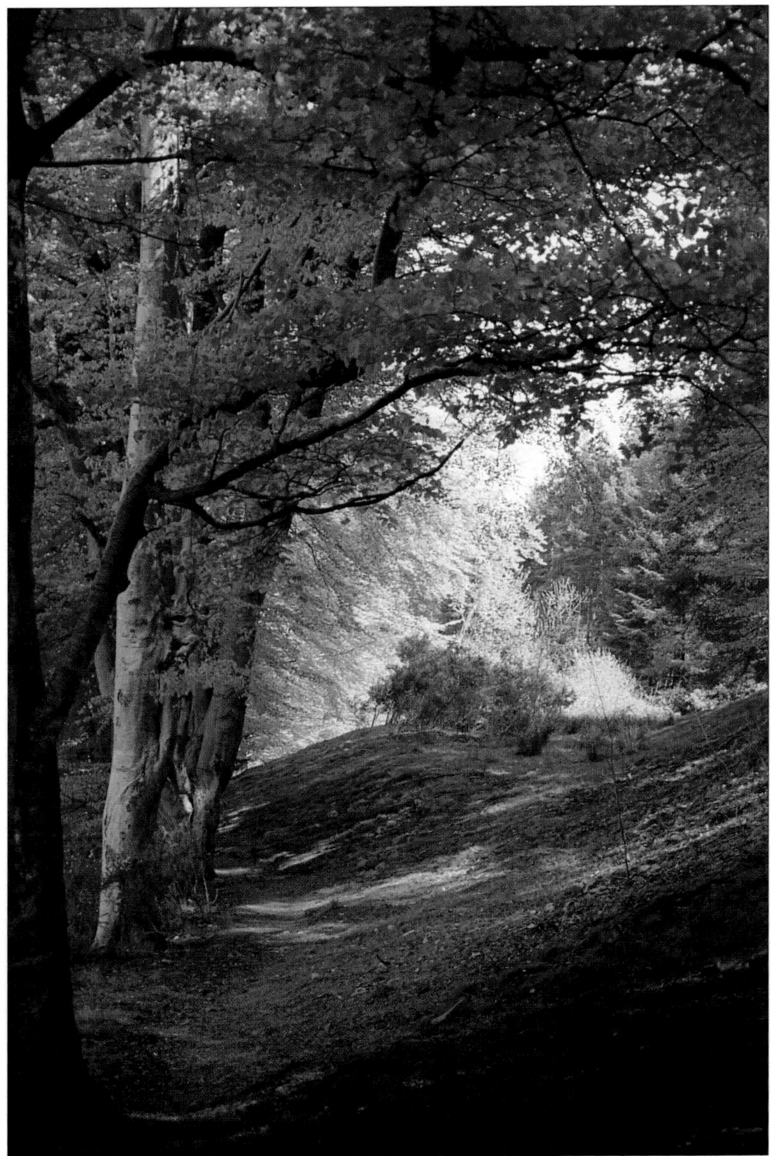

Woodland near Elrick Hill

turn left down steps to a burn.

Turn right alongside the burn – this is a most attractive part of the walk – and at a fork, take the left hand path to cross a footbridge over it. Initially the route continues along the right inside edge of the trees but the path swings left to a T-junction. Turn right through conifers and look out for where a waymarked post directs you to bear left off the main track to continue along a path.

The path bends left to head uphill, passing some of the items on the Sculpture Trail, curves left again – make sure that you keep on the main path all the while – and continues through a car park. Keep ahead, take the left-hand upper path at a fork and you finally descend to the start. ●

Scolty Hill

Start	Scolty Woodland Park, from Banchory cross bridge over River Dee and follow signs to Scolty Hill
Distance	3 miles (4.8km) Shorter version 2 miles (3.2km)
Approximate time	2 hours (1½ hours for shorter walk)
Parking	Scolty Woodland Park
Refreshments	None
Ordnance Survey maps	Landrangers 38 (Aberdeen, Inverurie & Pitmedden) and 45 (Stonehaven & Banchory), Pathfinder 258, NO69/79 (Banchory)

Although rising to the modest height of only 983ft (299m), the climb up to the monument on the summit of Scolty Hill is quite a steep one and even the fittest walkers will puff and pant a bit before they get there. The reward is a magnificent panorama of hills and forests, with particularly memorable views over Deeside. The full walk includes a short woodland circuit before ascending the hill; the shorter version goes straight for the summit.

The mixed woodlands of Scolty were mostly felled during the Second World War and the area was replanted after being acquired by the Forestry Commission between 1941 and 1954. It became a woodland park in 1993. Begin by heading across to the Scolty Woodland Park information board and just after passing it, turn left off the main track, at a yellow- and red-waymarked post, onto a path through conifers.

If following the shorter walk, keep ahead here along the main forest track and rejoin the full walk at point Ⓑ.

The path curves gently uphill to a T-junction. Turn right and continue uphill to reach the edge of the trees where you turn right Ⓐ and head up to re-enter woodland. At the next T-junction, turn sharp right along a track which later descends to another T-junction Ⓑ. Turn left at a sign to Scolty Hill – here rejoining the short walk – and head uphill to a kissing-gate. Go through and turn left, now following white waymarks for the rest of the walk. At the next sign to Scolty Hill, turn right to continue more steeply uphill, eventually emerging onto open heathery moorland and keeping ahead to the tower on the summit Ⓒ.

Scolty Tower was erected in 1842 as a memorial to General William Bennett of the Banchory Lodge Estate, a distinguished soldier. The views from here are magnificent and take in the Grampian Highlands, the eastern edge of the Cairngorms and Clachnaben, while below is Banchory and the winding River Dee.

At a fork just beyond the monument and triangulation pillar, take the right-hand path which winds quite steeply

The view from the slopes of Scolty Hill

downhill across moorland to a T-junction. Turn right to continue along the side of the hill, later re-entering woodland and descending gently to a kissing-gate. Go through, briefly rejoining the outward route, then continue walking downhill to a way-marked post Ⓑ. Here leave the outward route by keeping ahead along a straight, wide track to return to the start. ●

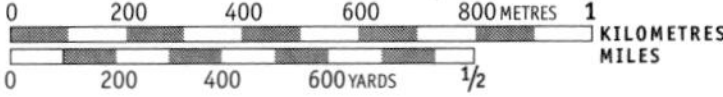

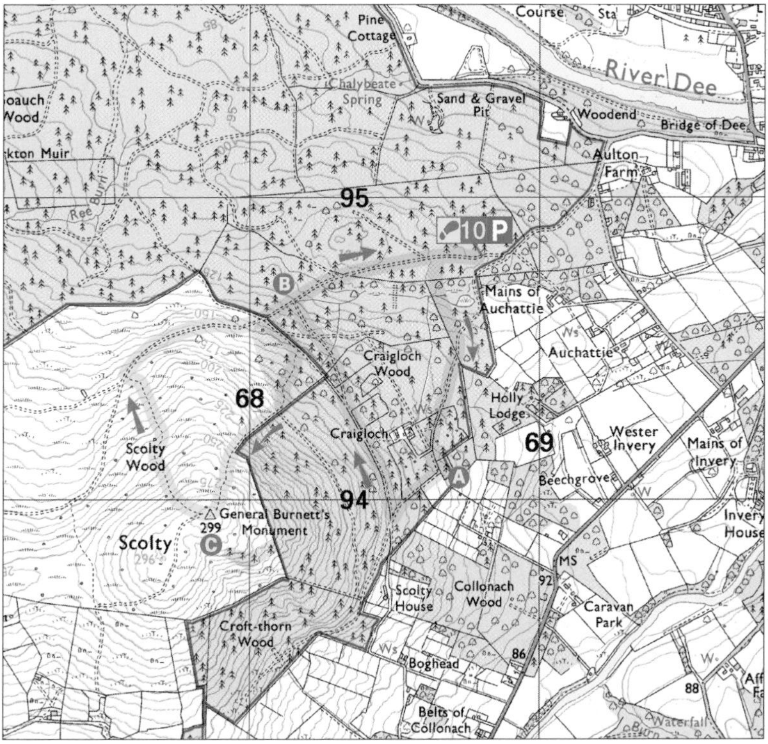

SCALE 1:25 000 or 2½ INCHES to 1 MILE 4CM to 1KM

Tap o'Noth

Start	Tap o'Noth car park, signposted from A941 1½ miles (2.4km) west of Rhynie
Distance	3 miles (4.8km)
Approximate time	2 hours
Parking	Tap o'Noth
Refreshments	None
Ordnance Survey maps	Landranger 37 (Strathdon), Pathfinder 213, NJ42/52 (Rhynie)

A short, steady, moderately steep – though not strenuous – ascent, on clear paths and tracks, leads to the 1851-ft (563m) summit of Tap o'Noth, site of an Iron Age Pictish fort. Both from the summit and on the descent, the views over the surrounding countryside are magnificent.

Tap o'Noth

Begin the walk by turning left out of the car park and heading uphill along an enclosed path to a stile. Climb it and keep ahead into trees, climb another stile and then turn left to continue steadily uphill through an area of gorse bushes.

The path later flattens out to reach a gate. Do not go through it but turn right Ⓐ and follow a worn grassy track, heading directly towards Tap o'Noth. Continue along a clear track across heathery moorland, climbing more steeply over the western flanks of the hill and bending right to continue up the southern slopes.

The village of Rhynie can now be seen below. The track finally swings left through the enclosure of the fort to the triangulation pillar at the summit of the hill Ⓑ.

The remains are those of an ancient Pictish hill-fort of uncertain date, but thought to have been constructed anytime between 1000BC and 1000AD. Archaeological excavations indicate that it comprised two enclosures that were built at different times, and some of the stones have been vitrified, fused together by intense heat. It is one of the highest forts in Scotland. The views from this point are both extensive and superb.

Return to the start by the same route, enjoying more grand views on the descent. ●

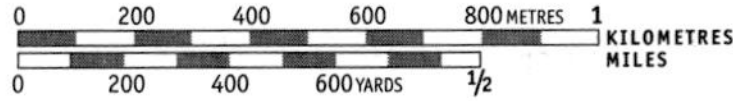

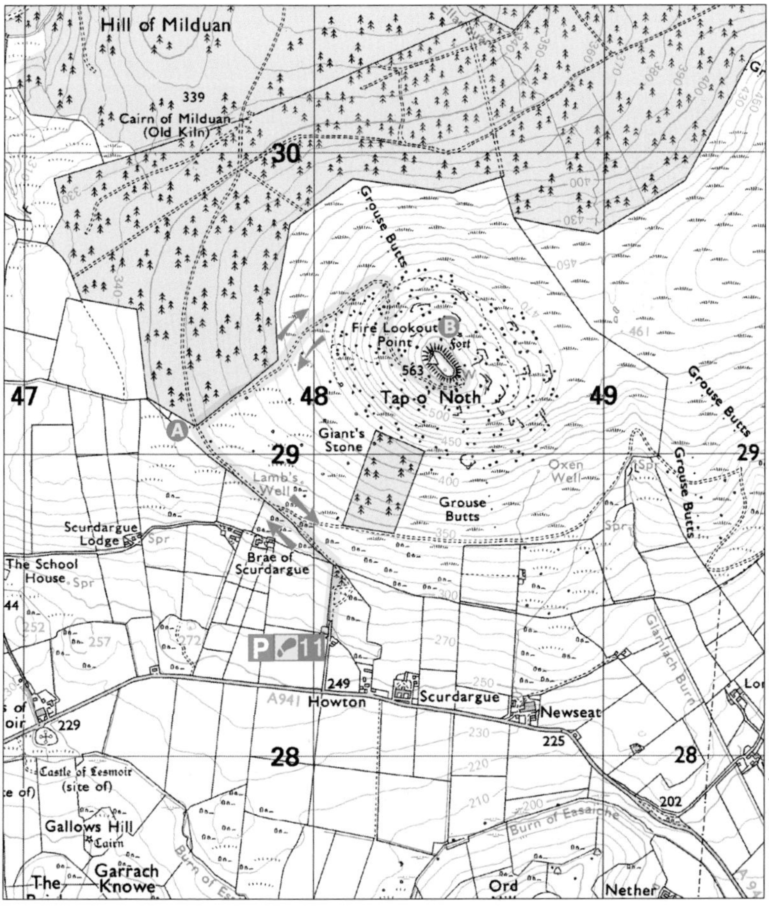

SCALE 1:25 000 or 2½ INCHES to 1 MILE 4CM to 1KM

Kemnay and the River Don

Start	Kemnay, Aquithie Road car park
Distance	5½ miles (8.9km)
Approximate time	2½ hours
Parking	Kemnay
Refreshments	Hotel at Kemnay
Ordnance Survey maps	Landranger 38 (Aberdeen, Inverurie & Pitmedden), Pathfinder 229, NJ61/71 (Kintore & Monymusk)

The outward route is mainly through the beautiful woodlands of the Fetternear Estate close to the west bank of the River Don. After crossing a suspension footbridge over the river, known locally as the Shakkin' Briggie (for obvious reasons), the return is mostly along quiet lanes high above the east bank. Throughout the walk there are splendid views up and down this attractive stretch of the Don.

The River Don near Kemnay

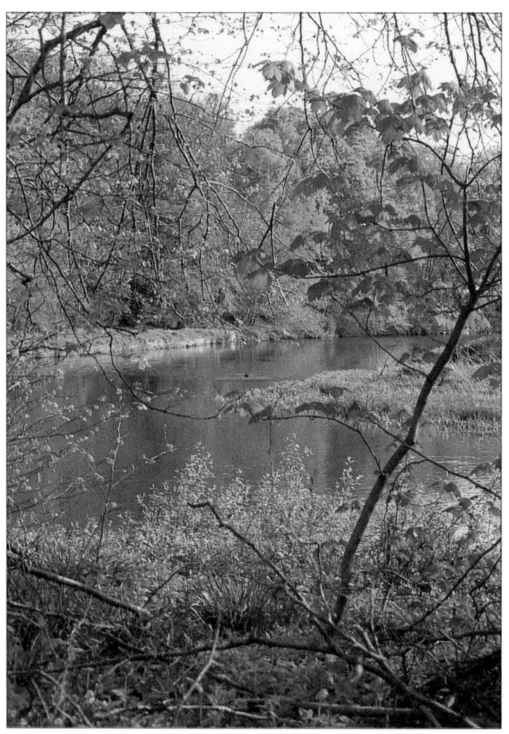

Turn right out of the car park and take the first road on the right, signposted to Fetternear. At a T-junction, turn right to cross the Bridge of Kemnay over the River Don and turn right along a tarmac track Ⓐ to go through the entrance gates to the Fetternear Estate.

Follow the track through woodland, later emerging from the trees and continuing by the attractive, tree-lined riverbank. After re-entering woodland, follow the river around a right bend and turn right to cross a footbridge over a burn. Continue along a rough track and over to the left the ruins of

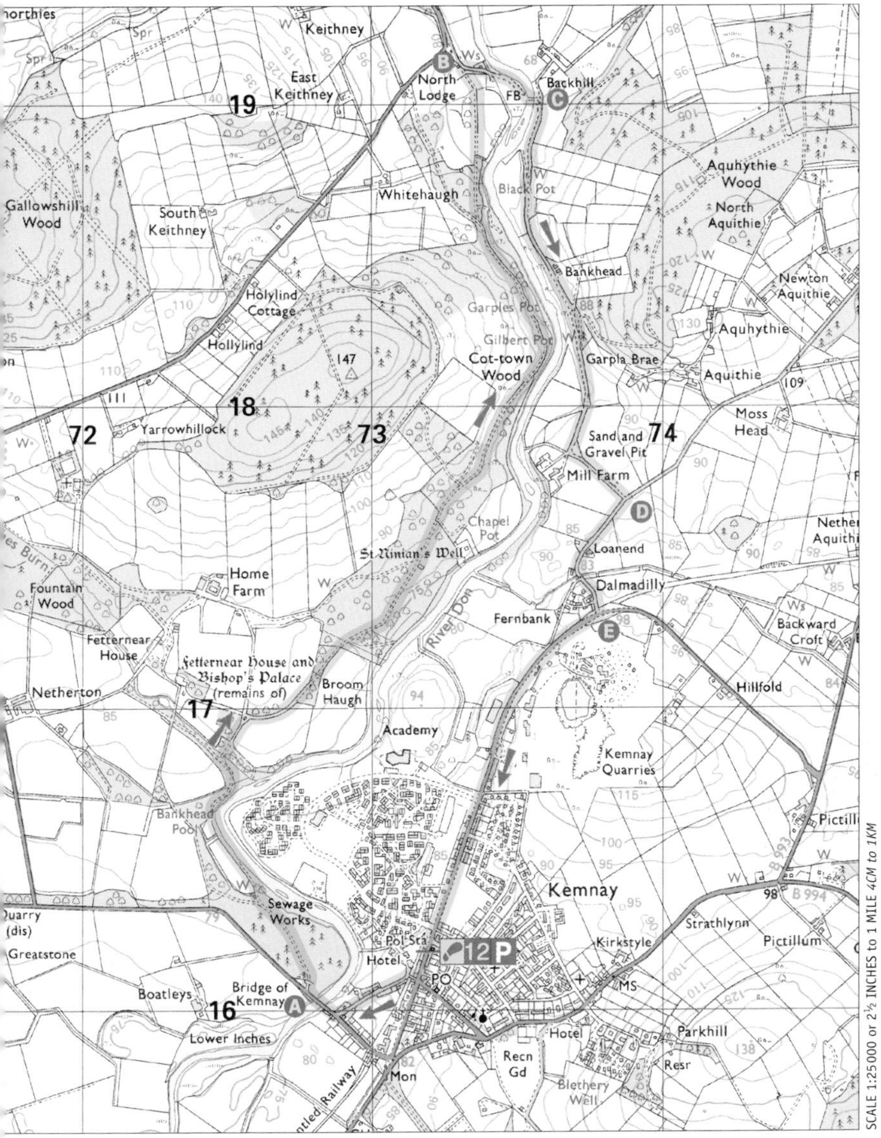

SCALE 1:25 000 or 2½ INCHES to 1 MILE *4CM to 1KM*

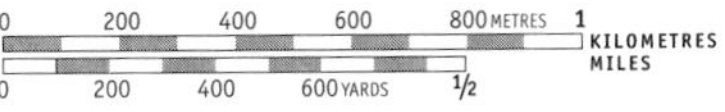

Fetternear House can be seen. This 16th-century house, built on the site of a medieval bishop's palace, was burnt down in 1919. At a fork, take the right hand track to a T-junction, turn right and continue along a tree-lined track, going through three gates. After the third gate, keep ahead across meadows and go through another gate to Whitehaugh Lodge.

Turn sharp right here **B** along a lane down to the river and where it ends, turn left to cross the Shakkin' Briggie over the River Don. Turn right head uphill along a path to a narrow lane **C** and keep along it high above the east bank of the river, following it around a left bend and heading gently uphill to a T-junction **D**. Turn right along a winding lane up to a road, turn right again **E** and follow the road back to the start, passing the entrance to Kemnay Quarry.

Cruden Bay and the Bullers of Buchan

Start	Cruden Bay
Distance	5 miles (8km)
Approximate time	2½ hours
Parking	Cruden Bay
Refreshments	Pubs at Cruden Bay
Ordnance Survey maps	Landranger 30 (Fraserburgh & Peterhead), Pathfinder 200, NK02/03/13 (Cruden Bay)

Much of the route is on a cliff top path along a particularly rugged and indented stretch of the Aberdeenshire coast. You walk around small coves and pass some spectacular stacks and rock arches, culminating in the Bullers of Buchan. Equally dramatic are the gaunt ruins of Slains Castle, seen just after the start of the walk. Expect to see (and hear) plenty of seabirds along the route, including – if you are lucky – puffins.

At the car park – which is in both sides of the road – face the church, turn right to the end of the car park and take the path ahead through woodland. The path crosses a burn, continues by it through a mini-gorge, ascends gently and curves left along the top of the cliffs to the stark and mysterious-looking ruins of Slains Castle. Despite its name, it is not a castle but a huge, rambling mansion built in 1836 for the earls of Errol. As Bram Stoker used to stay nearby, it may have been the inspiration for Dracula's castle. It was abandoned

Slains Castle on the Aberdeenshire Coast

in the 1920s and subsequently fell into ruin.

In front of the castle, turn left away from the sea across the end of the inlet of Long Haven and at a junction, turn right (A) along a straight, walled track. Go through a gate into a car park at a road corner, turn right (B) through another gate and walk along a path back towards the sea. Turn left to continue along a narrow and winding cliff-top path, passing the rocky island of Dunbury and the headland of the Grey Mare – both likely to be teeming with seabirds – and the path eventually turns sharply inland around the edge of the steep inlet of Robie's Haven.

Turn right to pass in front of cottages and keep ahead along the other side of the inlet to reach the rim of the Bullers of Buchan. (C) This rock formation, a dramatic and unusual sight, makes a natural amphitheatre and is usually teeming with seabirds. It is thought to be a cave whose roof collapsed.

Retrace your steps to the junction near Slains Castle (A) but instead of turning left to the ruins, turn right along a track for an alternative finale. The track enters woodland and eventually emerges onto a road. Keep ahead into Cruden Bay, turn left (D) along the main road and by the Kilmarnock Arms Hotel, turn left again to return to the start. ●

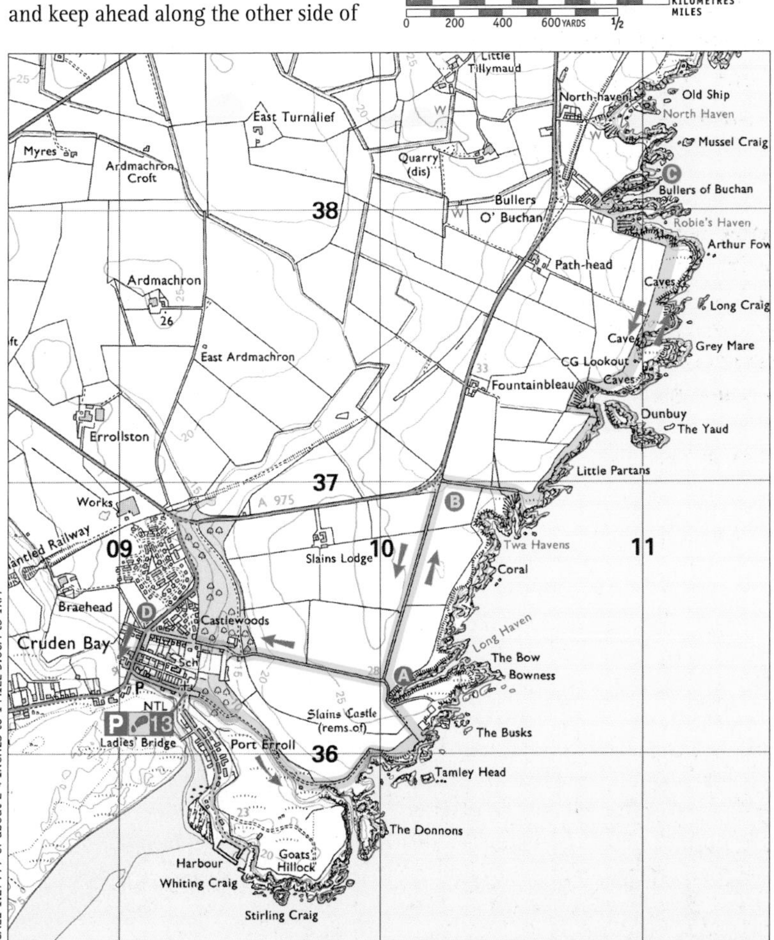

Duff House and the Bridge of Alvah

Start	Duff House, signposted from A98 on the outskirts of Banff
Distance	5½ miles (8.9km)
Approximate time	2½ hours
Parking	Duff House
Refreshments	Tearoom at Duff House, light refreshments at Montcoffer House
Ordnance Survey maps	Landranger 29 (Banff), Pathfinder 148, NJ56/66 (Banff & Cullen)

Much of this highly attractive route is through the woodland surrounding Duff House and there are fine views over the Deveron valley. Scenic highlights of the walk are the views of the river from the Bridge of Alvah, where the Deveron flows through a dramatic gorge, and the extensive views near the end looking across to Banff and the Moray Firth. Historic interest is provided by the splendid 18th-century house.

Like Haddo House (Walk 1), Duff House was also designed by the distinguished architect William Adam, and built in the 1730s. It was the home of the earls of Fife but is now a branch of the National Galleries of Scotland and has a fine collection of paintings, sculpture and furniture.

Start in front of the house and with your back to it, turn right along a path to a T-junction **A**. Turn left onto a tarmac drive along the right edge of playing fields and keep ahead through the Fife Gates to enter woodland. The gates were named after the 2nd earl of Fife who played a major role in laying out the park in the mid-18th century. At a fork take the left-hand track (passing beside a gate) and continue past a former ice house and the Duff Mausoleum; the latter built in the 1790s also by the 2nd earl. The track then heads gently downhill and at a junction keep ahead along the main track. At a fork, take the right hand main track again and at a T-junction in front of a house, turn left along a tarmac track, between woodland on the left and fields on the right.

The track re-enters woodland – there are some fine old beeches here and impressive views below to the left of the River Deveron – to reach another T-junction. Turn left onto a rough track which heads downhill to cross the Bridge of Alvah **B**, erected in 1772. This is a most dramatic spot where the river flows through an almost perpendicular gorge. Keep ahead to a

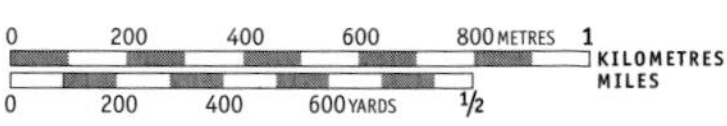

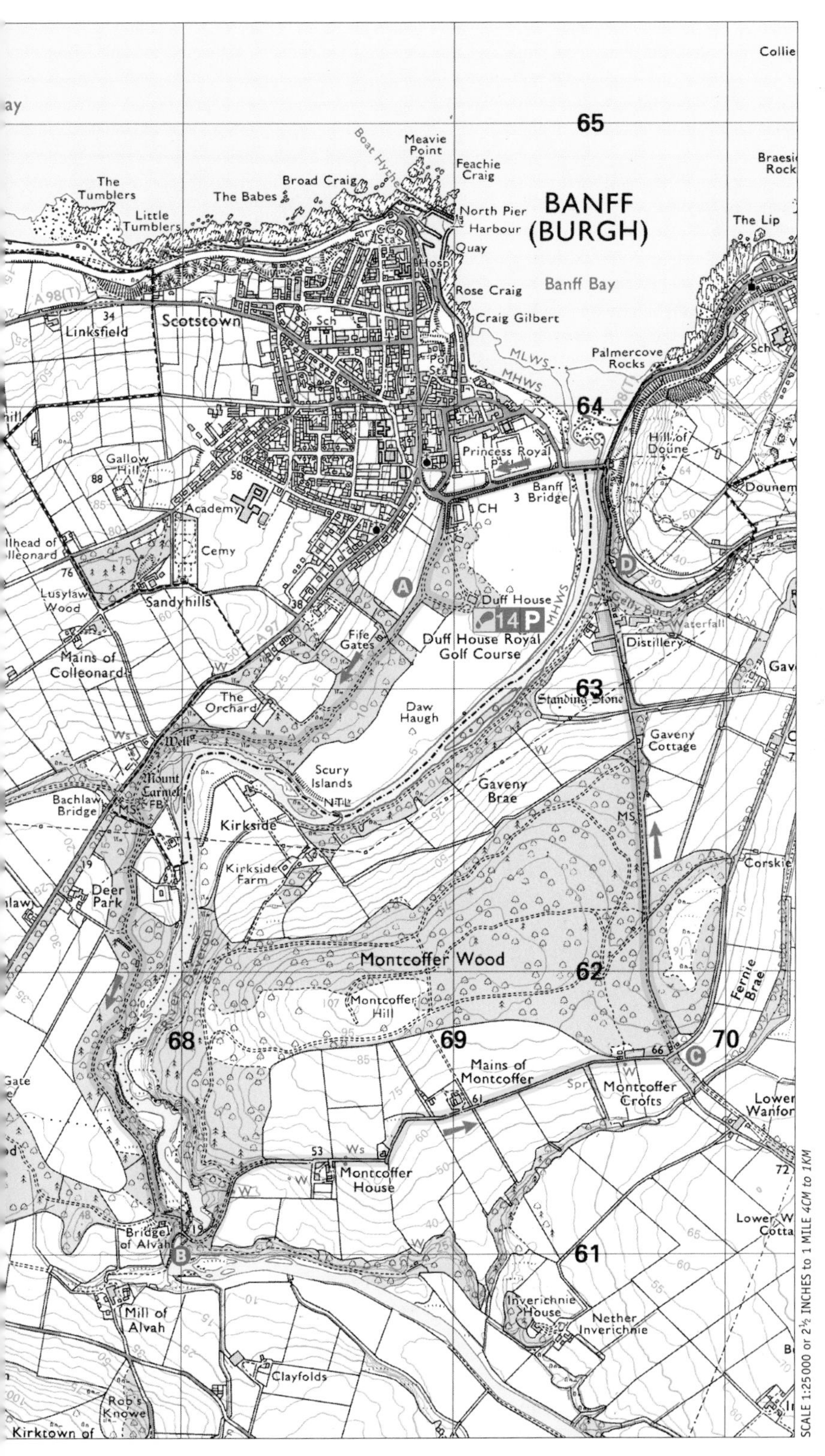
BANFF
(BURGH)
Banff Bay
Scotstown
Linksfield
Duff House
Duff House Royal
Golf Course
Montcoffer Wood
Montcoffer Hill
Mains of
Montcoffer
Montcoffer
House
Montcoffer
Crofts
Bridge
of Alvah
Mill of
Alvah
Kirkside
Mount
Carmel
Bachlaw
Bridge
Deer
Park
Scury
Islands
Daw
Haugh
Gaveny
Brae
Gaveny
Cottage
Distillery
Hill of
Doune
Inverichnie
House
Nether
Inverichnie
Clayfolds
Rob's
Knowe
Sandyhills
Academy
Fife
Gates
The
Orchard
Gallow
Hill
Mains of
Colleonard
Lusylaw
Wood
Meavie
Point
Feachie
Craig
North Pier
Harbour
Quay
Rose Craig
Craig Gilbert
Palmercove
Rocks
Broad Craig
The Babes
The
Tumblers
Little
Tumblers
Princess Royal
Banff
Bridge
Standing Stone
Waterfall
Fernie
Brae
The Lip
SCALE 1:25 000 or 2½ INCHES to 1 MILE 4CM to 1KM

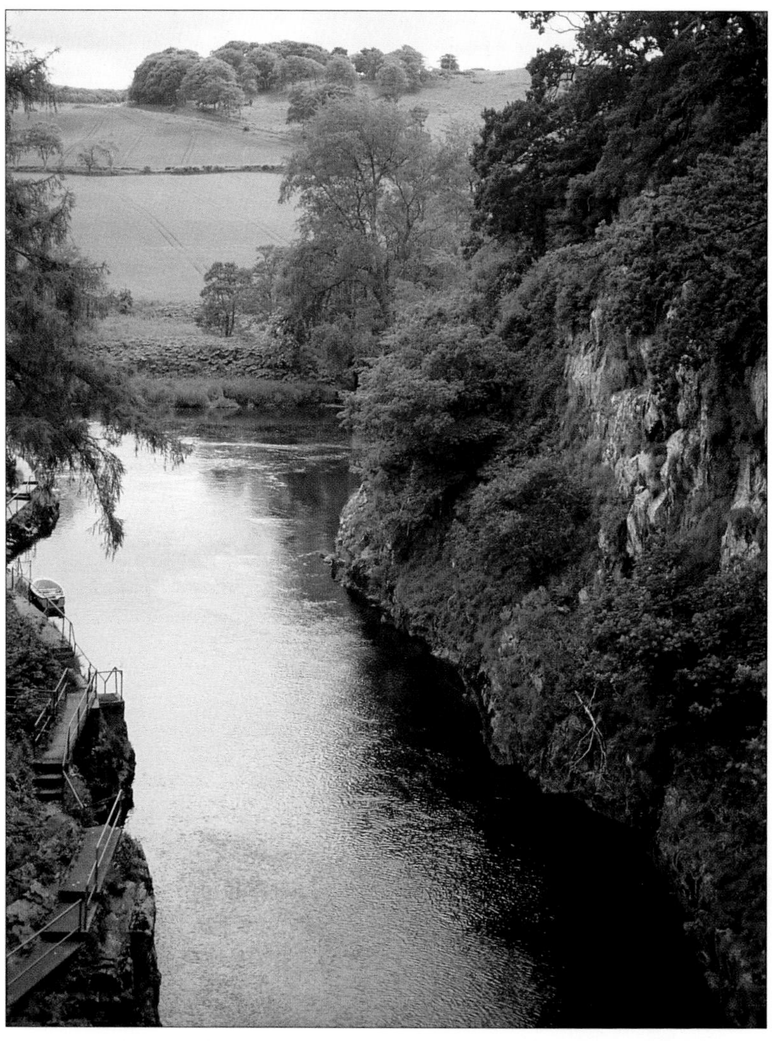

River Deveron at the Bridge of Alvah

fork and take the left-hand upper track which later curves right and heads uphill to Montcoffer House, formerly owned by the Russell family who lived at Aden House (Walk 6).

Continue past the house and after a left bend the track becomes a tarmac lane which you follow to a T-junction. Turn left, and then take the first track on the left Ⓒ and where the main track swings right to a house, keep ahead along a hedge-lined track. The track later re-enters woodland, heads gently downhill and on emerging from the trees, there is a superb view ahead over Banff and the Moray Firth, with Duff House seen over to the left. Continue downhill to the Macduff Distillery and follow a tarmac drive between the buildings and up to a road Ⓓ.

Turn left towards the coast and turn left again along the main road to cross the bridge over the Deveron. Keep ahead and where the road bends right into Banff, turn left along the drive to Duff House. At the corner of the playing field Ⓐ, turn left again to return to the start. ●

Above Balmoral

Start	Crathie church
Distance	5½ miles (8.9km)
Approximate time	2½ hours
Parking	Crathie church
Refreshments	None
Ordnance Survey maps	Landranger 44 (Ballater & Glen Cova), Pathfinder 256, NO29/39 (Ballater & Crathie)

This 'there and back' route in the heart of Royal Deeside takes you over the river and up into the hills above Balmoral. It is an easy walk, with a gentle and gradual ascent, and the reward is magnificent views over Deeside and the distant Cairngorms. On the descent, the tower of Balmoral Castle comes into sight. The walk can easily be combined with a visit to the nearby castle and grounds which are generally open to the public between April and July.

Crathie Church is famous the world over as the place where the Royal Family worship when staying at Balmoral Castle. It was built in 1893, replacing a more modest early 19th-century church which itself was a replacement for a medieval church passed soon after the start of the walk. The Balmoral Estate was purchased by Prince Albert for Queen Victoria in 1852 and was chosen both for its location and its climate, being considerably drier than some

River Dee near Balmoral

alternative sites in the Western Highlands. The castle, built in a neo-Gothic style to resemble a medieval fortress, was completed in 1855.

Start by taking the tarmac track at the side of the car park and by the tourist information centre which curves left and passes the remains of St Manir's Church, the 15th-century predecessor of Crathie Church. It remained in use until the end of the 18th century but needed repairs and was felt to be too small, hence a new church was built on a different site. John Brown, Queen Victoria's devoted servant, is buried in the adjacent graveyard.

Continue along the track to a

0 200 400 600 800 METRES 1 KILOMETRES
0 200 400 600 YARDS ½ MILES

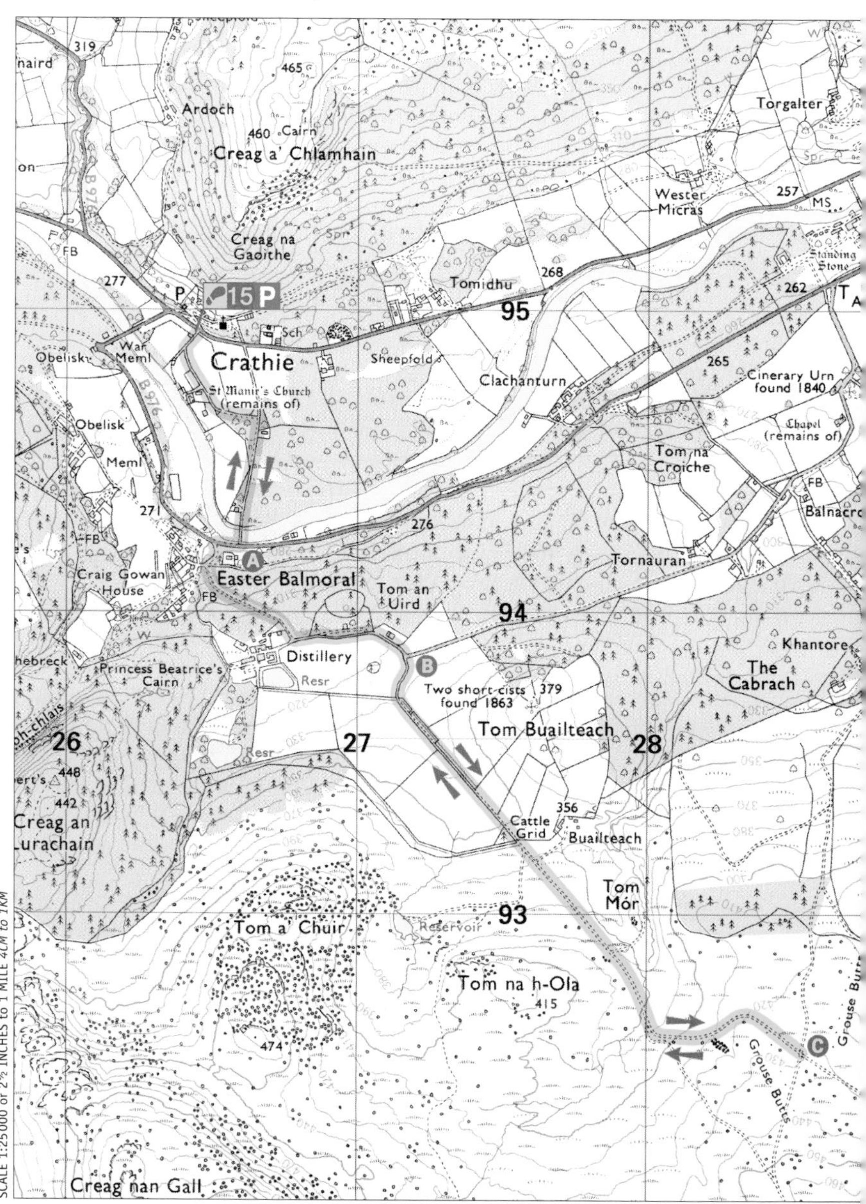

SCALE 1:25 000 or 2½ INCHES to 1 MILE 4CM to 1KM

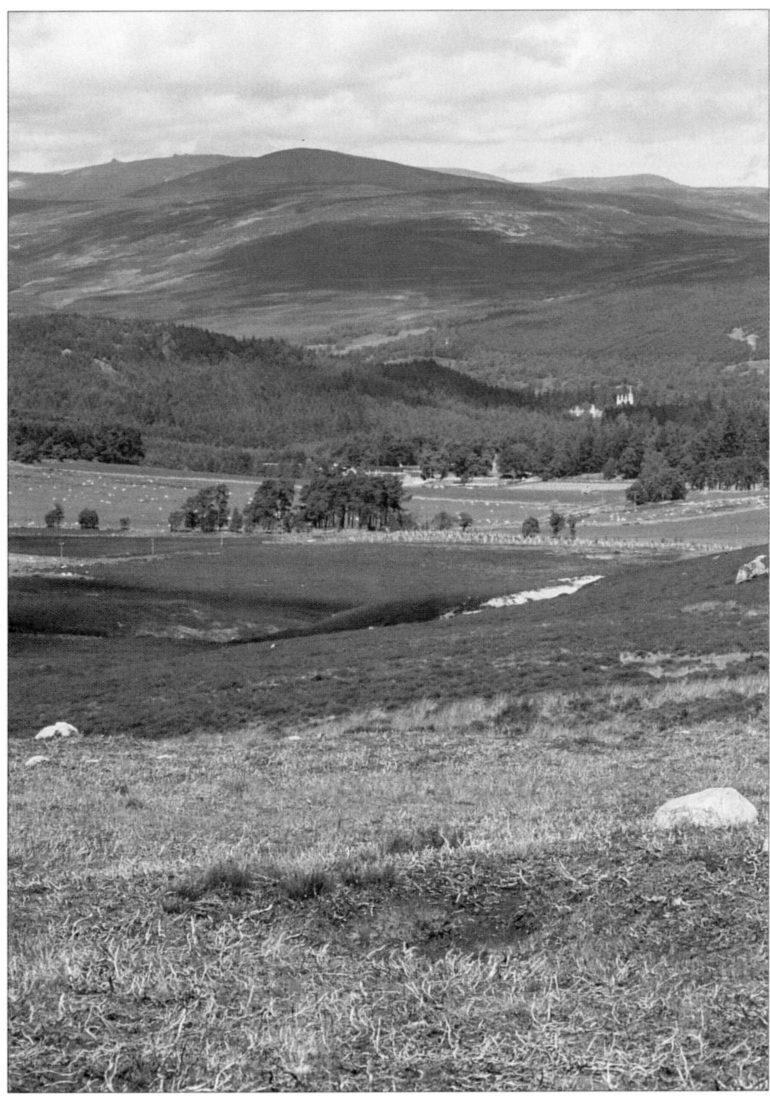

A view of Deeside from above Balmoral

T-junction, turn right and where the track ends, keep ahead along a path to cross a suspension footbridge over the River Dee. There are grand views both up and down the river. Turn right along a road Ⓐ, take the first turning on the left, signposted to the Royal Lochnagar Distillery, and the lane heads uphill and bears left to reach the distillery. At a T-junction turn left, follow the lane as it curves right and where it bends left, keep ahead along a gently ascending tarmac track Ⓑ.

After going through a kissing-gate, the track – now a rough one – continues across open heathery moorland, bending left and then curving right to go over a slight brow and reaching a crossroads of tracks Ⓒ. From here retrace your steps downhill to the start, enjoying more fine views over Deeside and the Cairngorms, with the top of the tower of Balmoral Castle in sight. ●

Collieston and the Sands of Forvie

Start	Collieston, Cransdale car park on north side of village
Distance	6 miles (9.7km)
Approximate time	3 hours
Parking	Cransdale car park
Refreshments	None
Ordnance Survey maps	Landranger 38 (Aberdeen, Inverurie & Pitmedden), Pathfinder 200, NK02/03/13 (Cruden Bay)

This outstanding coast walk takes you from the picturesque harbour of Collieston along a cliff-top path, across the heather, grass and dunes of the Forvie Nature Reserve, to the meagre remains of a 12th-century church. There are superb views along the coast, especially looking southwards across a huge expanse of sands to the buildings of Aberdeen on the skyline. A visit to the Forvie Centre near the end of the walk is well worthwhile.

The car park is based around Cransdale which, despite its close proximity to Collieston, was formerly a separate fishing community. Begin by taking the path, signposted to Harbour and Village, which passes around a small sandy cove and heads up into Collieston, passing in front of cottages to a road. Collieston was once a busy fishing village but declined in the 19th century when the industry became concentrated in the bigger harbours at Peterhead and Aberdeen.

Turn left down to the harbour, keep ahead along a path, passing in front of the toilet block, bear right to ascend steps and at a fork take the right-hand upper path – via more steps – on to a road. Turn left, at a T-junction turn left again and take the first turning on the right (A). Where the road ends, keep ahead along a track and at a fork, take the right-hand cliff path which winds above a bay called Perthudden to a kissing-gate (B). This admits you to the Forvie National Nature Reserve, one of the largest and least disturbed sand dune systems in Britain, managed by Scottish Natural Heritage. It is noted for its wide variety of plants and birdlife and has the largest breeding colony of eider ducks in the country.

At a junction of paths immediately after going through the kissing-gate, bear left to continue across dune, grass and heather. The path winds along the top of the cliffs – there are steps and boardwalks in places – and passes above the beautiful sandy beach at Hackley Bay. Ahead there are superb views of the vast expanse of sand and dunes stretching southwards towards the Ythan estuary and the high rise buildings of Aberdeen can be seen on the horizon.

At a path junction by a footpath sign,

keep ahead and the path soon bends right, descends and then keeps above a track on the left before curving right over the dunes to the sparse ruins of the 12th-century Forvie Church Ⓒ. The church is all that is left of the once thriving farming settlement of Forvie, which had become buried under the moving sands by the 15th century. In

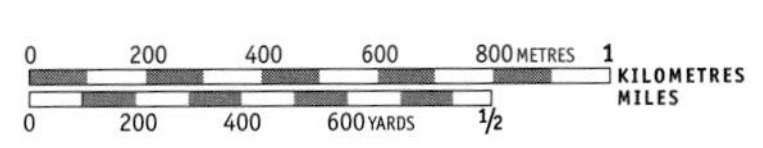

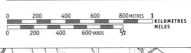

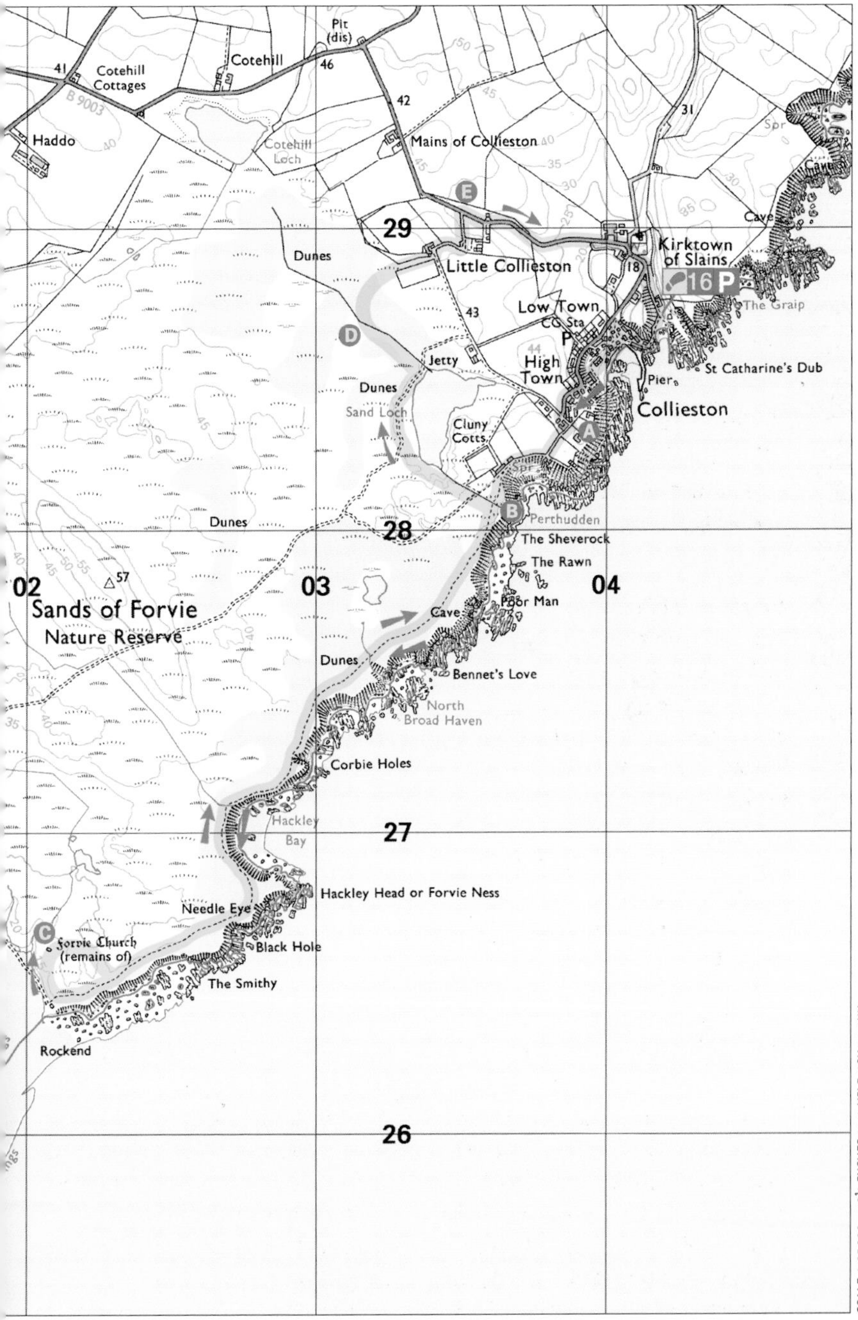

SCALE 1:25000 or 2½ INCHES to 1 MILE *4CM to 1KM*

the 18th century the sand front had also reached Collieston but since then has stabilised.

Just beyond the church, the path turns right to rejoin the previous route where you turn left and retrace your steps to the kissing-gate where you first entered the nature reserve Ⓑ. Do not go through it but turn left to walk along a winding path – more steps and boardwalks – which later curves right alongside Sand Loch and then bears left to continue roughly parallel to a wire fence on the right. Eventually the path bends right to a kissing-gate in the fence Ⓓ. Go through and take the path ahead to the Stevenson Forvie Centre. This opened in 1998 and contains displays and a wealth of information on the area.

Keep ahead along a tarmac drive which turns left to a road and turn right Ⓔ back towards Collieston, passing the church. At a fork on the edge of the village, take the left-hand tarmac track to return to the start. ●

Hackley Bay near Collieston

Inverbervie, Benholm and Gourdon

Start	Inverbervie
Distance	6½ miles (10.5km)
Approximate time	3 hours
Parking	Market Square in Inverbervie, alternatively use the Beach car park and start the walk from there
Refreshments	Pubs and cafés at Inverbervie, café at Mill of Benholm, pubs at Gourdon
Ordnance Survey maps	Landranger 45 (Stonehaven & Banchory), Pathfinders 273, NO87/88 (Stonehaven & Inverbervie) and 299, NO76/86 (Johnshaven)

The first half of the walk heads inland and follows a former coach road over the modest slopes of Gourdon Hill (446ft/136m) to Benholm. After passing the Mill of Benholm, the return route to Bervie Bay is along the coast, passing through the attractive fishing village of Gourdon. The walking is easy throughout and there are fine coastal views.

Begin in the Market Square in Inverbervie and turn left along the main street through the small town. (If starting from the Beach car park, turn left up Kirkburn to a T-junction and turn left along the main street).

The fishing harbour at Gourdon

Follow the road (A92) out of the town and after just over ½ mile (800m), turn right A, at a footpath sign to Benholm, along the track to Hallgreen Mains Farm. Take the first track to the left – there is another footpath sign to Benholm here – and head gently uphill over Gourdon Hill. This is an old coach road and there are fine views, both ahead along the coast and to the right over farming country. The track gently descends and finally emerges onto a lane at a bend B. Keep ahead if you wish to visit the church at Benholm; otherwise the route continues to the left, passing the Mill of Benholm. Parts of the building go back to the 18th century but there has been a mill on the site for at least 500 years. It remained in use until 1982 and has now been restored.

On reaching the A92 turn left and after about 100 yards (91m), turn sharp right C – almost doubling back – onto a tarmac track which bends left and later curves right to reach a T-junction by the cottages at Haugh of Benholm. Turn left D along a track by the shore and follow it into Gourdon, emerging onto a road. Continue past the harbour and through the fishing village to where the road peters out by the last of the houses. From here keep ahead along the coast path which bears left, following the curve of Bervie Bay, back to Inverbervie, a distance of about 1 mile (1.6km).

On approaching the town, the path bears left to join a track – a disused railway track which has been running parallel to the path since Gourdon – and continues along it to a road near the Beach car park. To return to the Market Square, turn left uphill E along Kirkburn to a T-junction in front of the church and turn right.

0 200 400 600 800 METRES 1 KILOMETRES
0 200 400 600 YARDS ½ MILES

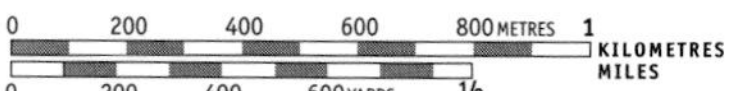

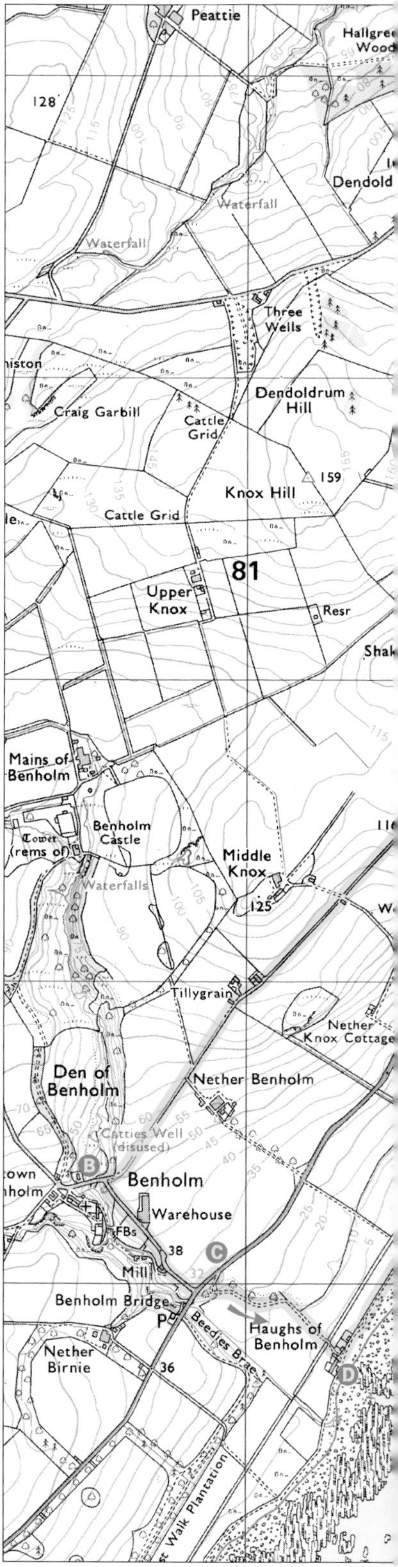

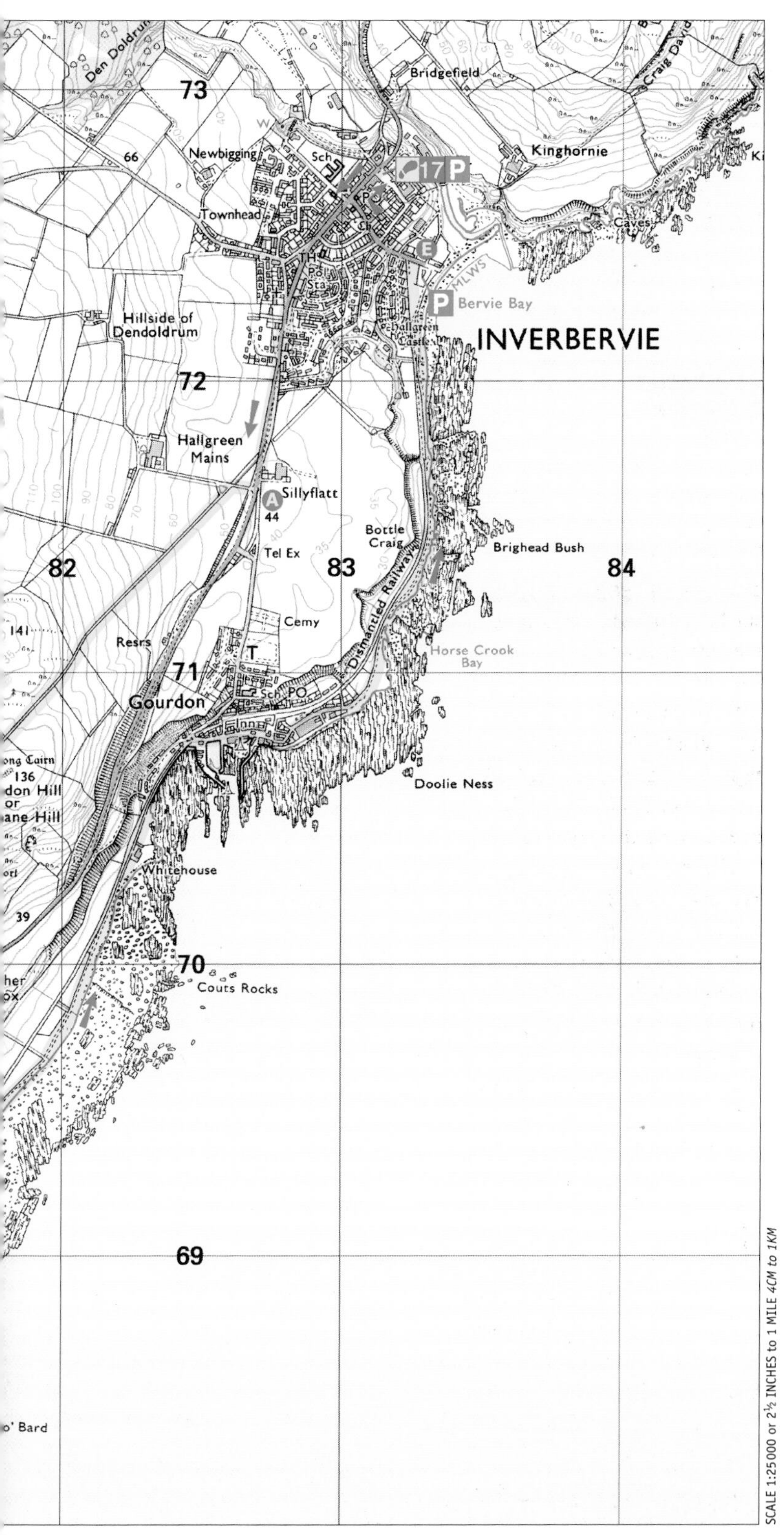

SCALE 1:25 000 or 2½ INCHES to 1 MILE *4CM to 1KM*

Crovie and Troup Head

Start	Crovie, car park and viewpoint just above the village
Distance	6½ miles (10.5km). Shorter version 4½ miles (7.2km)
Approximate time	3½ hours (2½ hours for shorter walk)
Parking	Crovie
Refreshments	None
Ordnance Survey maps	Landranger 30 (Fraserburgh & Peterhead), Pathfinder 149, NJ76/86 (Macduff)

Right from the starting point above the tiny and picturesque village of Crovie, there are extensive and spectacular views along the rugged coastline of the Moray Firth on this relatively energetic but most enjoyable walk. There are also fine views inland. The full walk includes a detour to the prominent 367-ft (112-m) high headland of Troup Head, a nesting place for thousands of seabirds.

Begin by walking down the steep, narrow lane towards the village of Crovie and where the lane bends sharply left **A**, keep ahead to descend a long flight of steps into the village. It is difficult to envisage that this tiny and remote place, hemmed in at the base of steep cliffs, was once a busy fishing harbour with a population of around 300. After a particularly fierce and destructive storm in 1953 much of the population of the village moved away and most of the cottages are now used as holiday homes.

After exploring the village, cross the footbridge opposite the bottom of the steps, turn right to head up a steep track and turn left at a T-junction. Continue along a track and at a fork **B**, take the left-hand lower track – there is a green-waymarked post here – which bends left to cross a burn and winds steeply uphill. To the left there are fine views across Gamrie Bay to Gardenstown, where the majority of Crovie's inhabitants relocated after the great storm of 1953. The winding track later levels off, passes a farm, bends right and becomes a tarmac lane which you follow to a T-junction **C**.

If following the shorter route, turn right at this point to omit the detour to Troup Head.

For the full walk, turn left up to a farm, turn left to pass between the farm buildings and then turn right to continue along a track. The track bends left, continues gently uphill and finally bends right to a gate. Go through and head gently uphill across a field to the triangulation pillar on Troup Head **D**. Walk on just beyond it for the best views and enjoy the sights and sounds of the seabirds.

Return to the junction of lanes **C** to rejoin the shorter route and keep ahead. Where the lane bends left by a farm, turn right, at a green-waymarked post, along the track to Stonewells **E**. The track bends first right, then bends left and heads up to the farm. Where the main track bends right into the farm, keep ahead along a fence-lined track which heads downhill – this stretch may be overgrown – bends sharply left and continues down to a gate. Go through, keep ahead to go through another and

Crovie

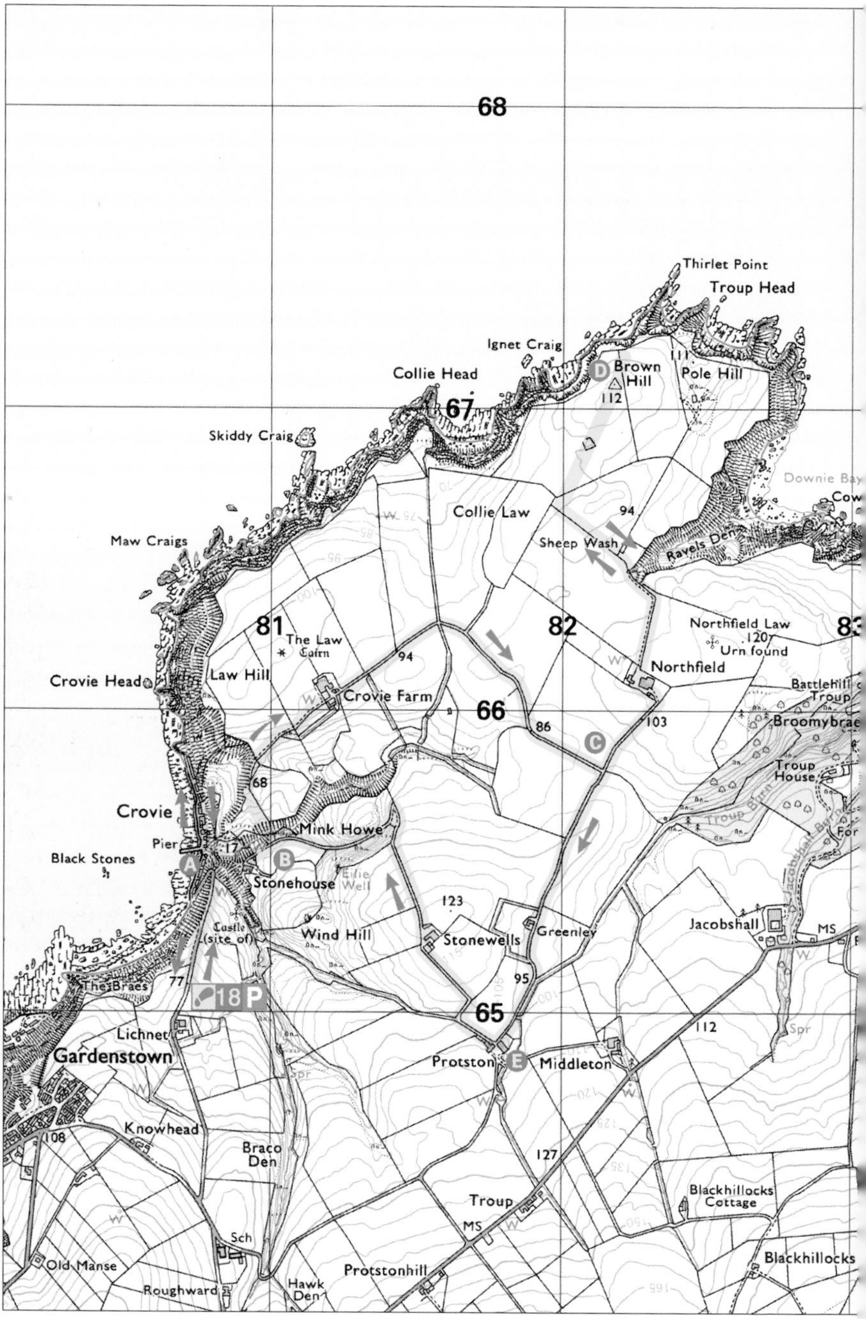

SCALE 1:25 000 or 2½ INCHES to 1 MILE *4CM to 1KM*

continue along the track, passing a house, to briefly rejoin the outward route.

Instead of following the outward route to the right down into Crovie, keep ahead along the track which bends right and heads up to a lane. Turn left and retrace your steps uphill to the car park.

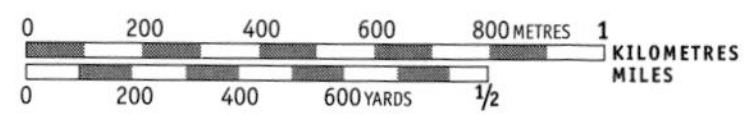

Deveron Valley

Start	Milltown of Rothiemay
Distance	7 miles (11.3km)
Approximate time	3½ hours
Parking	Roadside parking at Milltown of Rothiemay
Refreshments	Pub at Milltown of Rothiemay
Ordnance Survey maps	Landranger 29 (Banff), Pathfinder 181, NJ44/54 (Huntly [North])

The outward leg is mainly along a well-defined, high-level track above the river. After a brief descent through woodland, the return is along a lane. From many points on the route, there are fine and extensive views of the winding River Deveron and across the valley to the surrounding hills.

Deveron Valley

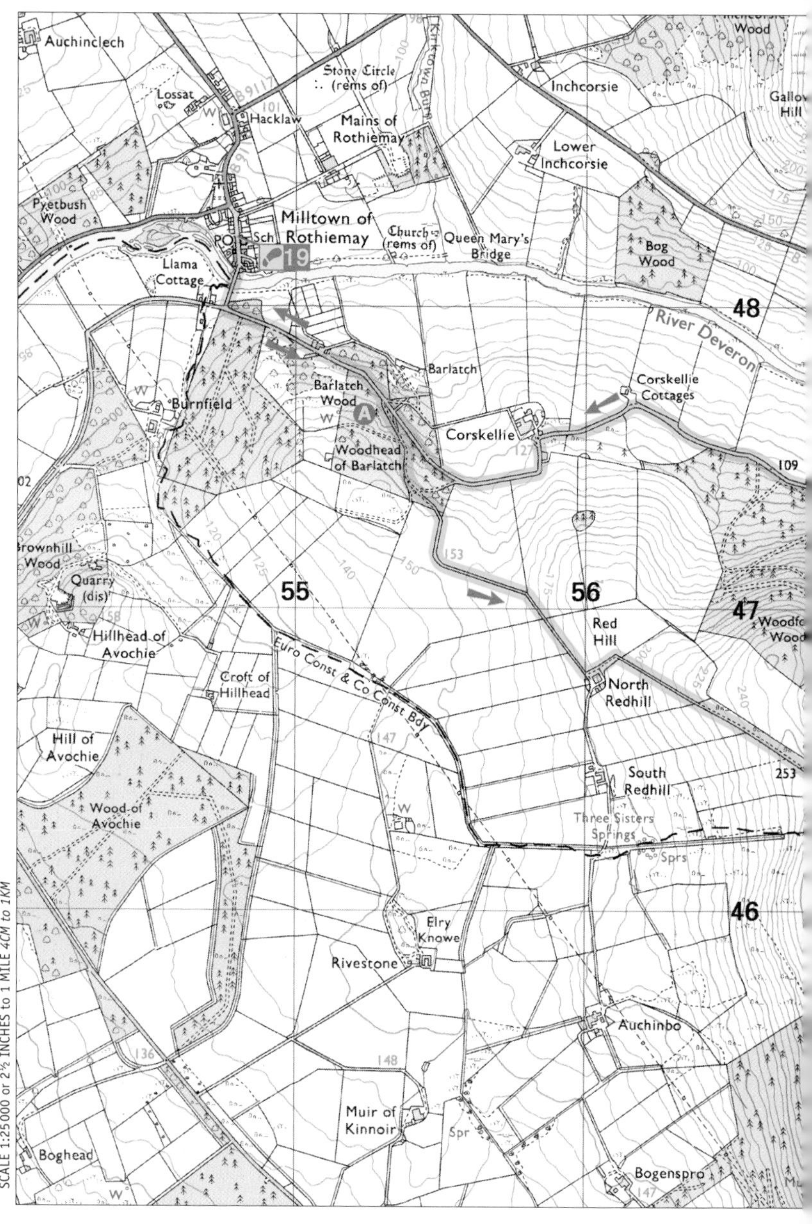

Start in the main street at Milltown of Rothiemay and walk down it, passing the post office and Forbes Arms Hotel, to cross the bridge over the River Deveron. At a T-junction, turn left along a lane which heads uphill and soon after entering conifer woodland, bear right onto the tarmac track to North and South Redhill Ⓐ. Continue uphill and at the top you emerge from the trees into open country and keep along the winding track to North Redhill Farm. In front of the farm buildings, turn left onto a rough track which bends right and heads uphill over the shoulder of Fourman Hill. As you continue along the track, going through two gates, there are grand views to the

0 200 400 600 800 METRES 1 KILOMETRES
0 200 400 600 YARDS ½ MILES

left over the valley of the winding River Deveron.

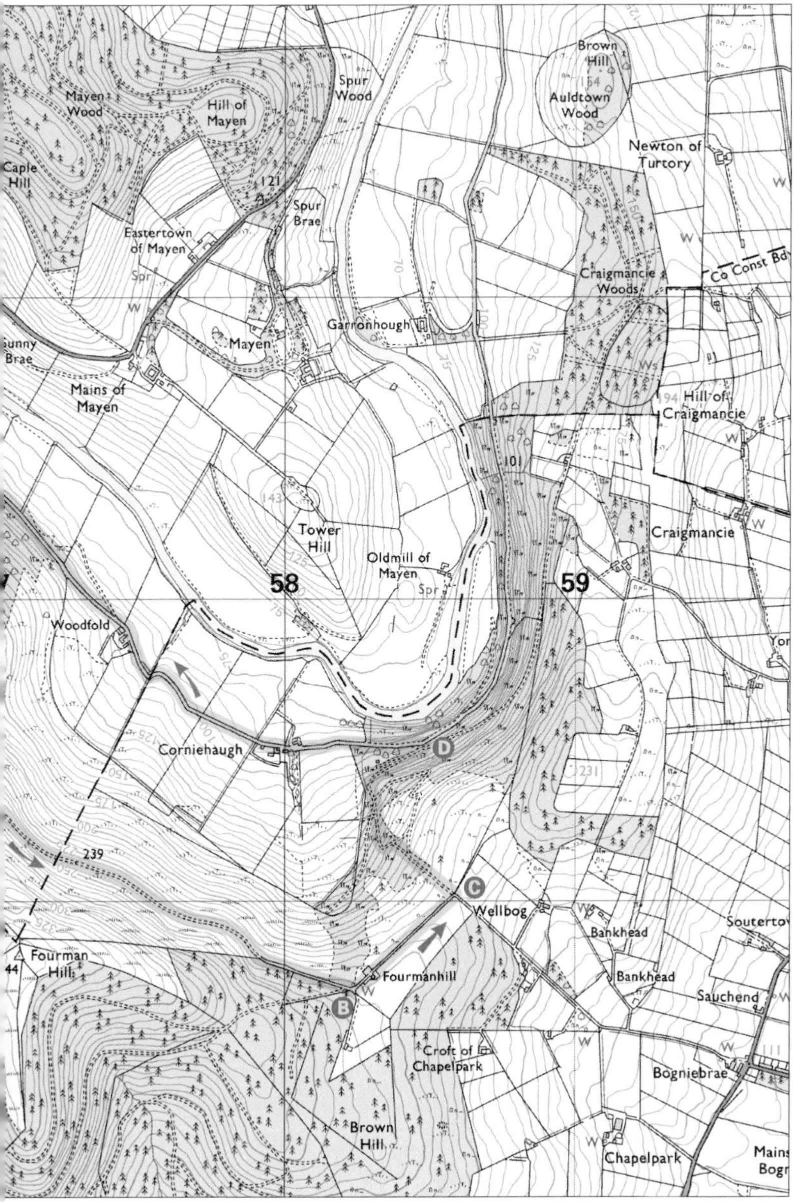

The track eventually emerges onto the end of a tarmac drive B. Turn left and where the drive turns right, turn left through a gate C and head downhill across a field. At the bottom of the field, follow the track to the right and continue steeply downhill through woodland. The track bends right, continues downhill and finally bends sharply to the left to go through a gate onto a lane D.

Turn left and follow the quiet, winding lane for about 3 miles (4.8km) back to Milltown of Rothiemay. ●

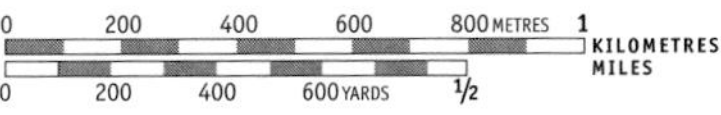

Elgin, River Lossie and Quarry Wood

Start	Elgin, in front of the cathedral
Distance	7 miles (11.3km)
Approximate time	3½ hours
Parking	Elgin
Refreshments	Pubs and cafés at Elgin
Ordnance Survey maps	Landranger 28 (Elgin & Dufftown), Pathfinder 146, NJ16/36 (Elgin)

From the splendid ruins of Elgin Cathedral, you walk along the banks of the River Lossie through parkland, crossing and recrossing the river several times, to the edge of Quarry Wood which occupies a hillside on the west of the city. Then follows a circuit of this attractive woodland, which includes passing the highest point from which there is an extensive view looking northwards to the Moray Firth coast. On the descent there are more fine views over the city. This is an undemanding walk with only one gentle climb through Quarry Wood.

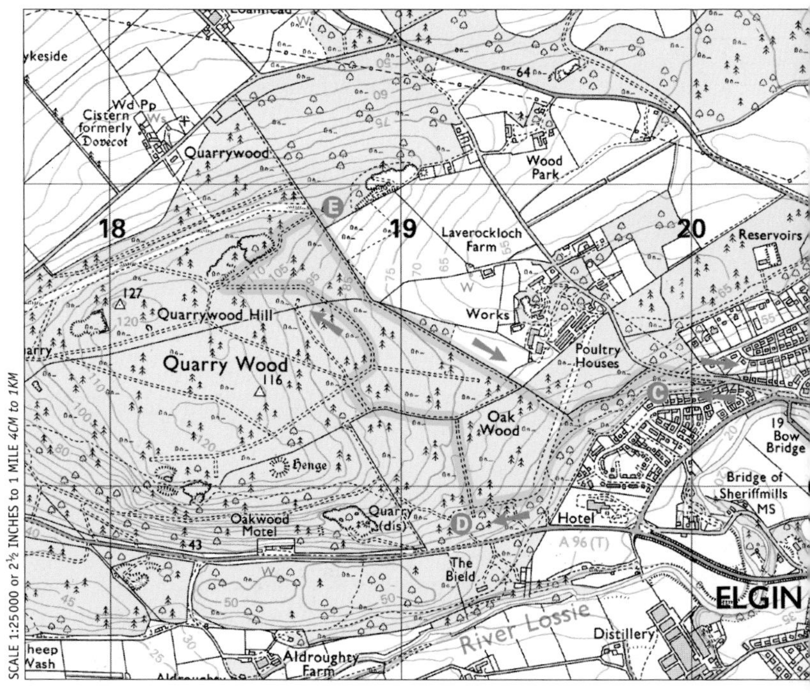

Elgin Cathedral, once one of Scotland's finest medieval cathedrals, is still beautiful and impressive even in ruin. It was founded in 1224 as the seat of the bishops of Moray but suffered several misfortunes. It was partially destroyed by fire in 1270 and then had to be largely rebuilt after being sacked by the 'Wolf of Badenoch', a brother of Robert III in 1390. After the upheavals of the Scottish Reformation and the abolition of the bishops, it fell into ruin, a process accelerated by the fall of the central tower in 1711 which destroyed the nave and north transept.

The remains comprise the west front with its twin towers, south transept, east end and chapter house. The quality of the architecture, particularly the 13th-century east end, ranks with that of any of the great English cathedrals.

With your back to the west front of the cathedral, turn right and then right again, by the remains of the 16th-century Bishop's House, to pass between the Biblical Garden on the left and the north side of the cathedral on the right. The Biblical Garden, appropriately adjacent to the cathedral, is made up of plants and sculptures based on the Bible and has a paved walkway laid out in the shape of a Celtic cross. It is well worth a visit.

Cross a bridge over the River Lossie and turn left onto a riverside path, later heading across grass away from the river to join a tarmac track. Bear left along it, shortly turn left to recross the Lossie and take the path ahead across Cooper Park. Keep ahead at a crossroads of paths to join a broad track and continue by the river again, passing to the left of one bridge and under a second one, here picking up a riverside path. The monument seen on the hill to the left is of a 19th-century duke of Gordon.

Follow the river around a loop to reach a road where you turn right Ⓐ to

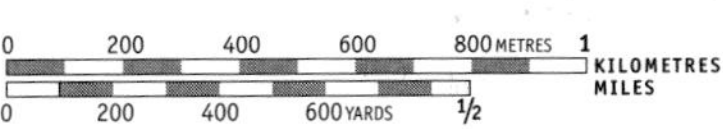

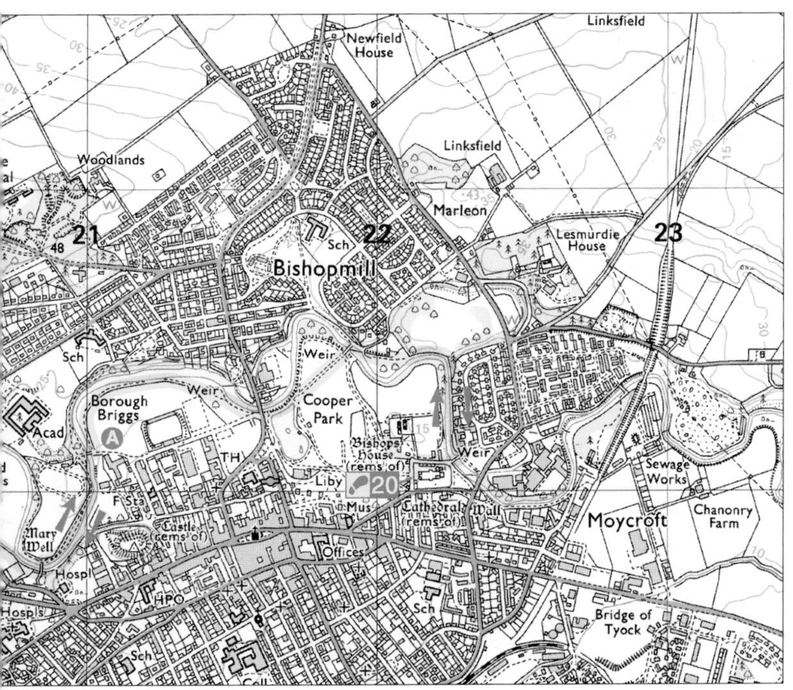

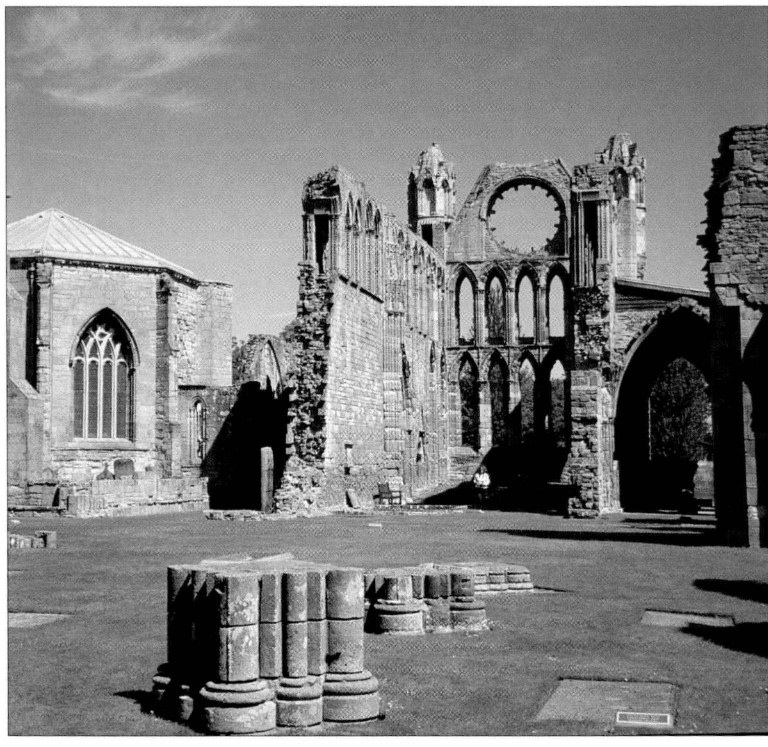

The remains of Elgin Cathedral

cross a footbridge. Turn left onto a delightful, tree-lined riverside path and turn left over the next footbridge. Turn right on the other side, follow the path to a road B and turn right to pass the Old Mills. These were formerly known as the King's Mills and are the oldest mills on the river. The road bends right, crossing the 17th-century Bow Bridge, the oldest bridge over the Lossie, to reach a T-junction. Turn left along Morriston Road, take the first turning on the right and turn left to head uphill along Brumley Brae.

The road enters woodland and where it bends slightly right, turn left onto a broad track C and pass beside a barrier to continue along a path through Quarry Wood. After about ½ mile (800m) – at a crossroads in a slight dip – turn right D and at a T-junction, turn left onto a well-surfaced path. Take the first path on the right which soon turns right, later curves left and follow it to the next T-junction. Turn right to reach a crossroads where there is a notice which tells you about Quarry Wood and its history. Much of Elgin was built from stone quarried here.

Turn right again and over to the left you soon come to a magnificent viewpoint E looking northwards to the Moray Firth, with a lighthouse visible on the skyline and Duffus Castle seen in the middle distance. At the viewpoint, turn right onto an attractive path which heads gently downhill along the left edge of the wood, with more fine views to the left over Elgin and the surrounding countryside.

The path later re-enters the trees to reach a crossroads. Turn left, here picking up the outward route, and retrace your steps through the wood, down Brumley Brae and beside the Lossie to return to the start. ●

Forest of Deer

Start	Drinnie's Wood and Observatory car park, signposted from A950 near Aden Country Park
Distance	7 miles (11.3km) Shorter version 4½ miles (7.2km)
Approximate time	3½ hours (2 hours for shorter walk)
Parking	Drinnie's Wood and Observatory
Refreshments	None
Ordnance Survey maps	Landranger 30 (Fraserburgh & Peterhead), Pathfinders 166, NJ85/95 (New Pitsligo & Strichen) and 183, NJ84/94 (New Deer & Maud)

The attractive conifer woodlands of the Forest of Deer spread over a low ridge and from their fringes there are a series of fine and extensive views over the gently undulating countryside of Buchan. The most outstanding viewpoint is the top of the Observatory tower, built by a local eccentric Victorian landowner, which is passed near the end of the walk. The full route takes in a circuit of White Cow Wood and from its northern edge, there are more fine and open views, dominated by the bulk of Mormond Hill, noted for its white horse.

Turn left out of the car park along a tarmac track which soon bends right and becomes a rough track. Follow it around a left bend and keep ahead along the left edge of the trees. This track was part of a racecourse laid out in 1845 for the eccentric Admiral George Ferguson of Pitfour. He also built the Observatory visited near the end of the walk, possibly in order to watch the races. After 1 mile (1.6km) you reach a junction of tracks, turn left **A** along a straight track to emerge onto a road opposite White Cow Wood car park **B**.

Turn left along the road for the short walk.

For the full walk, cross over into the car park, turn right beside a barrier and take the path ahead through the wood. At a junction, keep ahead gently uphill, follow the path around a right bend and continue on the main path all the time which winds through the trees, later curving left to emerge from them. The route then continues along the right edge of the wood and over to the right are particularly fine views of Mormond Hill, which has a white horse carved on its slopes.

The path later curves left **C** to continue the circuit of White Cow Wood and you keep along this path as far as a yellow-ringed post. Turn left at a T-junction and then at the next T-junction turn right – here rejoining the earlier route – and retrace your steps through the car park and onto the road to join up with the shorter walk **B**.

Turn right along the road and after nearly ¾ mile (1.2km), turn left onto a track by Auchmachar Lodge **D**. Go through a gate to re-enter the forest and keep along the main track through it. The track later turns left, at a fork take the main left-hand track and the Observatory can now be seen ahead on the skyline. Head down into a dip and up again and at the top, pass the first track on the left, keep ahead at a crossroads and then turn left onto a path.

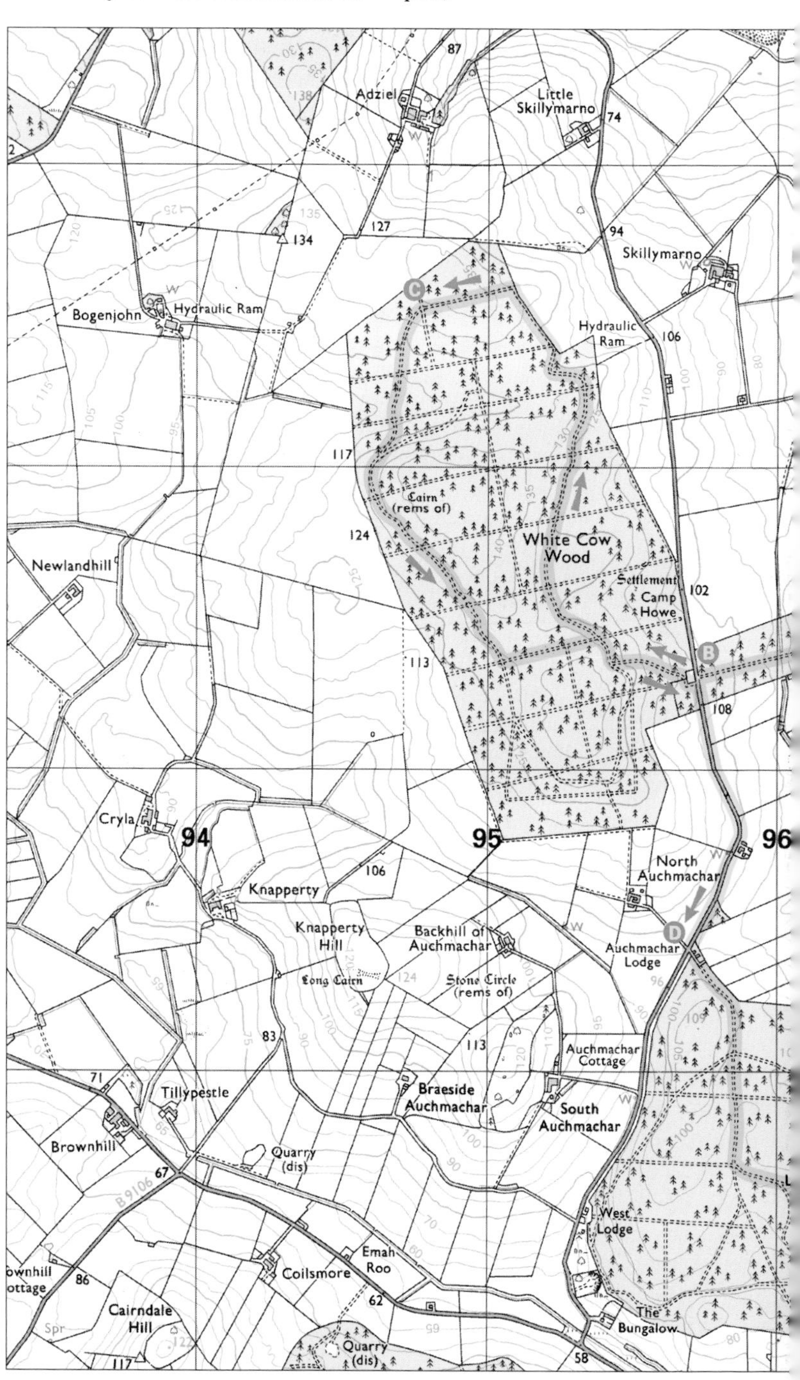

Head gently uphill between gorse bushes, curving gradually left, and a short path on the left leads up to the Observatory E. This octagonal tower was built in 1845 by Admiral George Ferguson and a spiral staircase inside leads to a viewing platform. The all-

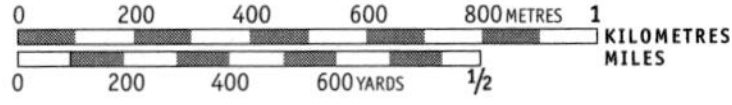

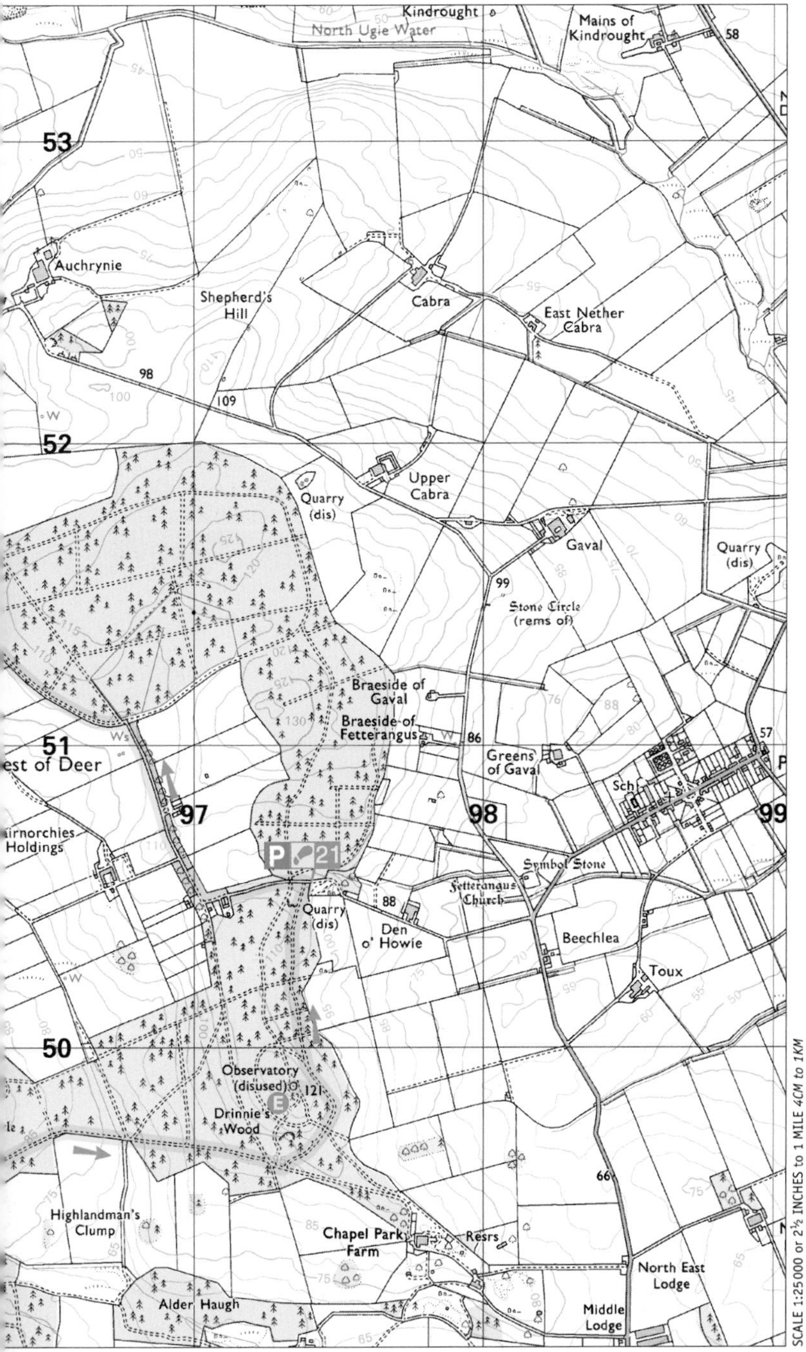

SCALE 1:25 000 or 2½ INCHES to 1 MILE *4CM to 1KM*

round views from here, across the Buchan countryside to the Grampian Highlands, are superb and include – in clear conditions – the well-known landmarks of Ben Rinnes, Tap o'Noth and Bennachie. Information panels give full details.

Retrace your steps from the Observatory to return to the main path, turn left – it has now widened into a track – and this track then leads directly back to the car park.

The Observatory, Forest of Deer

The Bochel and Crombie Water

Start	Tombae Quarry, take minor road that leads off from B9008 just to the north of Tomnavoulin and car park entrance is about ¾ mile(1.2km) along that road opposite a church
Distance	6½ miles (10.5km)
Approximate time	3½ hours
Parking	Tombae Quarry
Refreshments	None
Ordnance Survey maps	Landranger 36 (Grantown, Aviemore & Cairngorm), Pathfinder 212, NJ22/32 (Glenlivet)

This walk is amidst the glorious landscape of Glenlivet, which lies between the Ladder and Cromdale Hills at the north-east edge of the Cairngorms. It takes you through the valley of Crombie Water and includes a circuit of the lower slopes of the Bochel, a prominent hill which rises to 1610ft (491m). The views are superb and most of the route is on well-defined tracks and paths, although there are a few wet and muddy stretches. It is one of a series of excellent waymarked trails provided by the Glenlivet Estate.

The Glenlivet Estate, part of the Crown Estate, comprises around 58,000 acres (23,000 hectares) of heather-covered hills, woodlands and sheltered glens between the two broad straths of the Avon and Livet rivers. It was acquired by the Crown Estate in 1937. Start by walking back down the track to the lane and Catholic church (built in 1829) and turn left. At a waymarked post – G Walk 10 – by the drive to a house, Ⓐ climb a stile, head down a track and at a fork, continue along the right-hand track which bends right alongside the River Livet. The whole of the route is waymarked with regular G Walk 10 signs.

Turn left to cross Tullich Bridge over the river, continue along the track and at a waymarked post, turn right and walk across grass to a stile. Climb the stile, cross a footbridge over Crombie Water, turn left and climb another stile. Keep along the left field edge at the top of an embankment that slopes steeply down to the burn, later descending slightly – there are boardwalks here – to a stile. Climb it, keep ahead and at the next waymarked post Ⓑ, turn left to descend steps and recross Crombie Water.

Head across a field to enter woodland, climb steps and the path turns right to continue through heather, ferns and trees. On joining a track, turn right and the track later emerges from

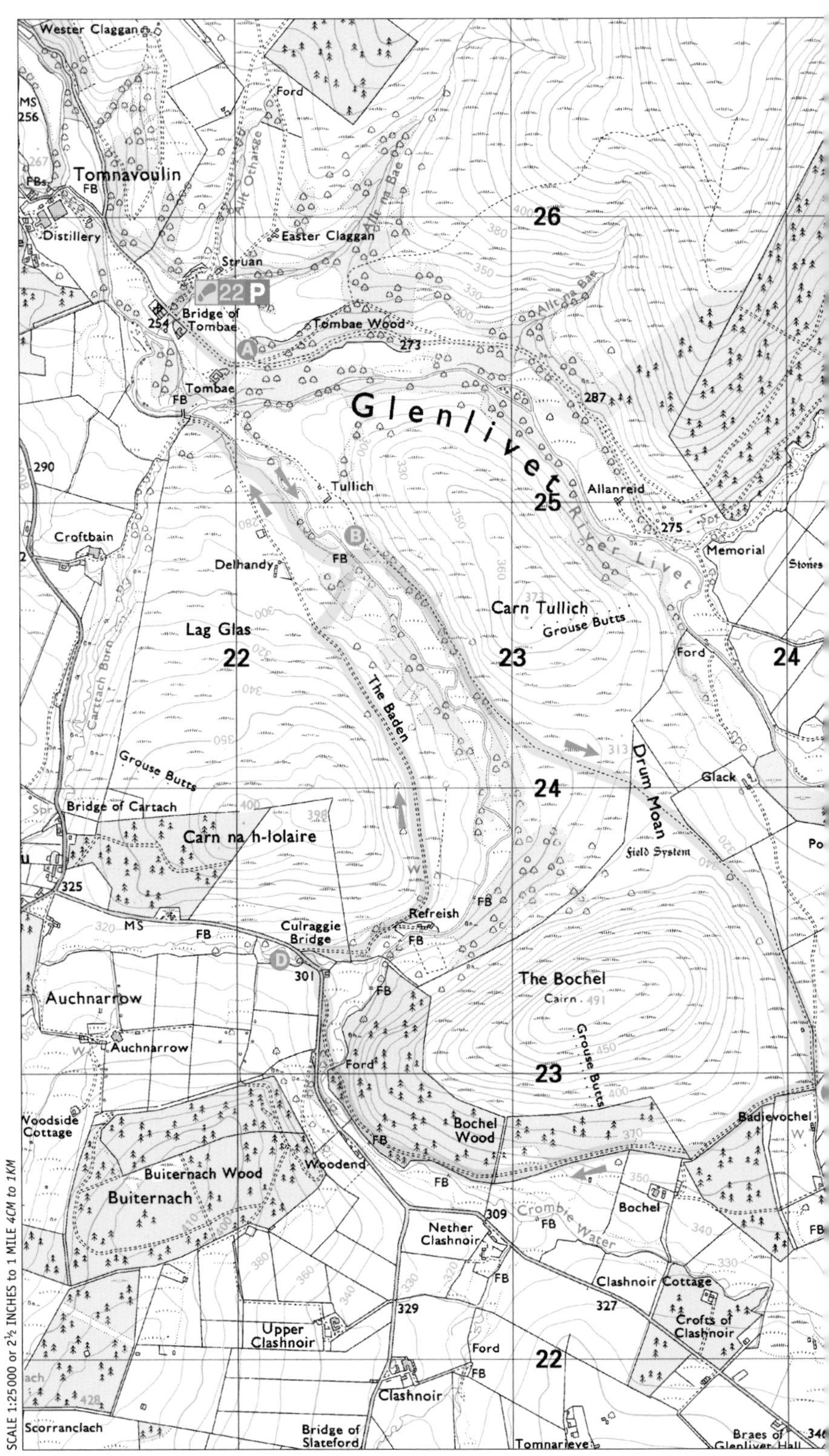

Wester Claggan
MS 256
Tomnavoulin
FBs
FB
Distillery
Ford
Allt Ochaisge
Allt na Bae
Easter Claggan
Struan
22 P
Bridge of Tombae
254
Tombae Wood
273
A
Tombae
Glenlivet
26
400
380
350
330
300
287
290
Tullich
Allanreid
25
River Livet
275
Memorial
Stones
B
Croftbain
Delhandy
Lag Glas
Carn Tullich
373
Grouse Butts
22
23
Ford
24
Cartach Burn
The Baden
313
Drum Moan
Glack
Grouse Butts
Bridge of Cartach
398
Carn na h-Iolaire
Field System
325
Refreish
MS
Culraggie Bridge
D
301
The Bochel
Cairn 491
Auchnarrow
Ford
450
Woodside Cottage
Bochel Wood
Badievochel
Buiternach Wood
Buiternach
Woodend
Crombie Water
309
Bochel
Nether Clashnoir
Clashnoir Cottage
327
Crofts of Clashnoir
329
Upper Clashnoir
22
Clashnoir
Scorranclach
Bridge of Slateford
Tomnarieve
Braes of Glenlivet Hall
428
SCALE 1:25 000 or 2½ INCHES to 1 MILE 4CM to 1KM

Glenlivet

the trees to continue uphill across open, heathery moorland to a gate and stile. The prominent bulk of the Bochel is over to the right. After climbing the stile, keep ahead towards a gate in a fence, do not go through it but turn right **C** alongside the fence to another stile. Climb that and continue across the lower slopes of the Bochel, later keeping parallel to a fence and track on the left, to a stile. Over to the left are striking views of the Ladder Hills.

Do not climb the stile but turn right – still following the contours of the hill – and you later keep by the edge of a conifer wood to reach a stile at a fence corner. After climbing it, take a narrow path into the conifers which later broadens into a clear track and heads downhill to a stile. Climb it – and another one immediately ahead – and continue down through the trees to emerge from them at a gate and stile. Climb the stile, continue along the track to climb another and keep ahead to a lane.

Turn right and after descending into a dip, turn sharp right over a stile **D** and walk along a track, climbing another four stiles. After the fourth one, look out for where a waymarked post directs you to turn right and head downhill across a field. At the next post, turn left to climb a stile and keep ahead, by a wire fence on the left. In the field corner turn right, head downhill – still alongside a fence – climb a stile, turn left and descend steps to another one.

After climbing that one **B** and heading up steps, you rejoin the outward route and retrace your steps to the start.

0 200 400 600 800 METRES 1 KILOMETRES
0 200 400 600 YARDS 1/2 MILES

Creag Choinnich and the Lion's Face

Start	Braemar, car park just off Glenshee Road
Distance	4½ miles (7.2km). Shorter version 3½ miles (5.6km)
Approximate time	2½ hours (2 hours for shorter walk)
Parking	Braemar
Refreshments	Hotels and cafés at Braemar
Ordnance Survey maps	Landranger 43 (Braemar & Blair Atholl), Outdoor Leisure 3 (The Cairngorms)

The shorter walk is basically a circuit of the woodland around the base and on the lower slopes of Creag Choinnich, a prominent hill that lies just to the east of Braemar. The full walk includes a climb to the 1765-ft (538-m) summit – a short, steep ascent but well worth the effort for the superb and extensive views of Morrone, the Cairngorms and both up and down Deeside.

The popular Deeside resort of Braemar, lying amidst hills on the eastern edge of the Cairngorms, is an excellent walking centre. Every September the famous Braemar Gathering takes place, a festival featuring Highland games, dancing and pipe bands. Opposite the car park where the walk begins are the scanty remains of the medieval Kindrochit Castle.

Start by climbing the steps from the car park onto the main road, turn left and at a footpath sign to 'Queen's Drive, The Cromlins and Creag Choinnich', turn right along Hillside Drive, passing to the left of a church. On approaching woodland – and where the road curves slightly right – turn left to climb a ladder stile into the wood. At a footpath sign, keep ahead, in The Cromlins and Creag Choinnich direction, and the path heads uphill to a waymarked post Ⓐ.

Turn left here if doing the short walk which avoids the ascent of Creag Choinnich.

For the full walk, keep ahead more

Braemar and Upper Deeside

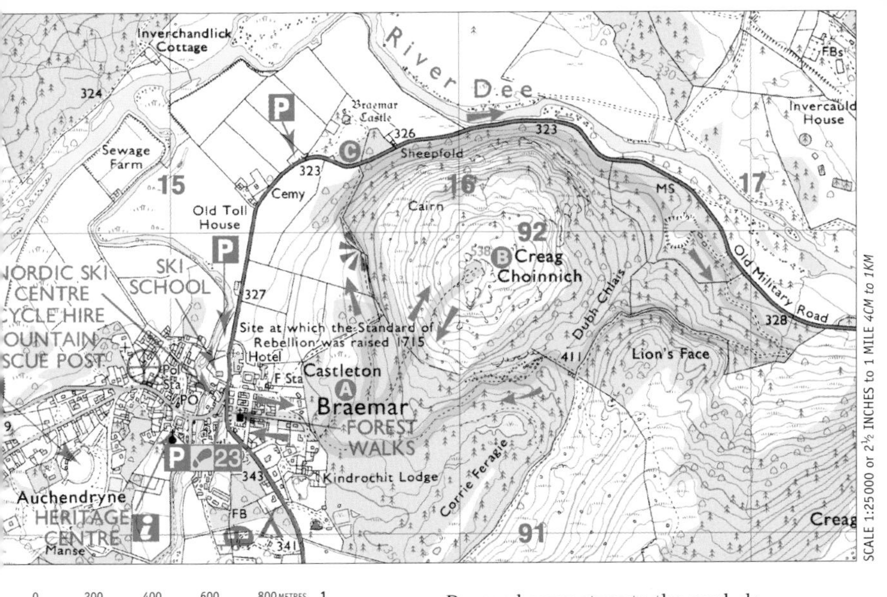

steeply uphill. On emerging from the trees, continue along a steep, rocky path through heather to reach the cairn on the summit of Creag Choinnich Ⓑ. At a height of 1765 feet (538m), the all-round views from here are magnificent. Immediately below is Braemar backed by the bulk of Morrone, there are long views both up and down Deeside and of Glenshee, and grand vistas of the Cairngorms.

Take care on the steep descent back to the junction of paths Ⓐ and turn right to rejoin the shorter route, now following yellow-ringed posts. The path contours around the wooded hillside to a ladder stile. Climb it, continue along the left edge of the trees and after descending steps, the path bends right. To the left across the road Braemar Castle can be seen. Although there was an earlier fortress on the site, the present castle was built in 1628 by the earl of Mar and was later transformed into a palatial residence by the Farquharson family. It now boasts a fine collection of furniture and paintings.

Descend more steps to the road, do not pass through the gate onto it – unless visiting Braemar Castle – but turn right Ⓒ through another gate and take the path that keeps along the bottom edge of the trees parallel to the road. There are attractive views over the River Dee as the route continues through the woodland above road and river. Later you follow the yellow-ringed posts through a council depot – where the vehicle track bends left to the road, keep ahead through trees again.

The path bends right, heads uphill and just after crossing a bridge over a burn, turn sharp right and continue uphill, recrossing the burn and heading up to pass a rock face called the Lion's Face. This is supposed to look like the face of a lion but the resemblance is hard to see. However it is another superb viewpoint.

Continue along the path but look out for where a footpath sign to Braemar directs you to turn right, now following a green-waymarked route. The path bears left through a wall gap, contours around the hillside and gently descends to a footpath sign and stile. Climb the stile, here rejoining the outward route, and retrace your steps to the start. ●

Suie Hill and Knock Saul

Start	Suie car park, on minor road between Clatt and Bridge of Alford
Distance	5½ miles (8.9km)
Approximate time	3 hours
Parking	Suie car park
Refreshments	None
Ordnance Survey maps	Landranger 37 (Strathdon), Pathfinder 213, NJ42/52 (Rhynie)

This 'there and back' walk on the Correen Hills follows the well-waymarked Gordon Way across the open moorland of Suie Hill, through the conifers of Whitehaugh Forest and up to the 1351-ft (412-m) summit of Knock Saul. There are a number of ascents and descents – though none are lengthy or strenuous – pleasant walking through woodland and over heather moorland, and extensive views from the higher points.

Start at the Gordon Way footpath post and take the grassy path through trees that passes along the left of the car park. The Gordon Way is a 12-mile (19-km) waymarked trail that runs from here to the Bennachie Centre.

Emerging from the conifers, the route continues across the open, heathery moorland on Suie Hill, at 1361ft (415m) slightly higher than Knock Saul but a less prominent hilltop. It is still a fine viewpoint, with

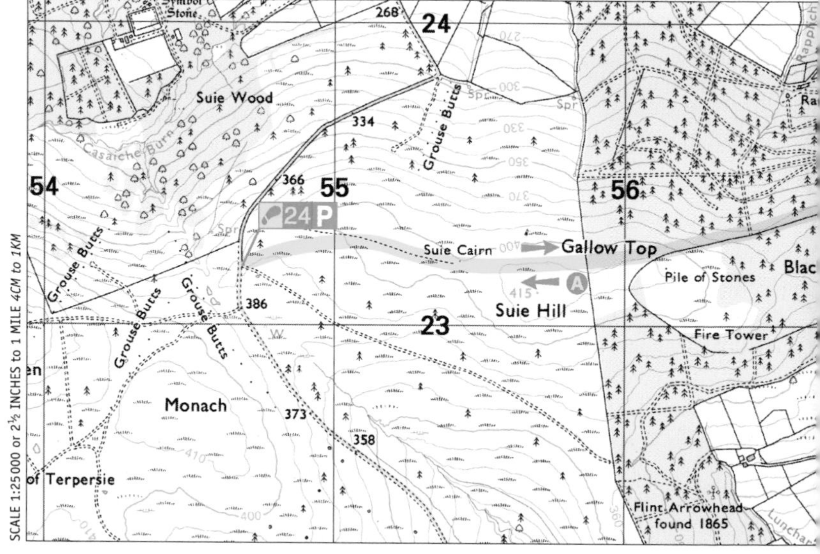

A view of Tap o'Noth from Knock Saul

Tap o'Noth visible on the skyline. Go through a gap in a largely redundant fence, keep ahead across the moorland and the path heads downhill along the right edge of woodland and then enters the forest Ⓐ. Continue downhill, curving left to reach a track, turn right

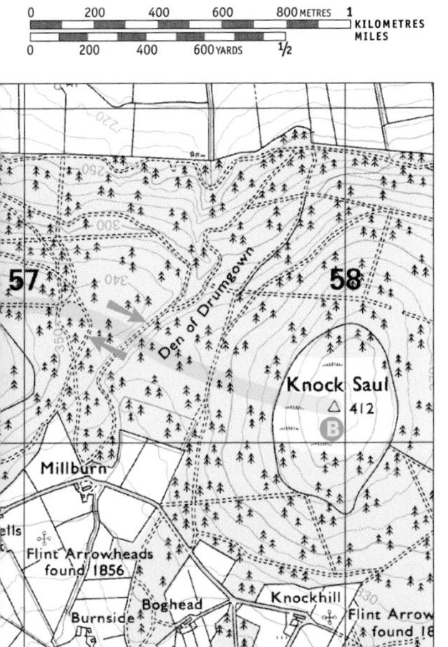

uphill and at a Gordon Way sign, turn left onto a narrow path which winds uphill across a felled area. At the next Gordon Way sign, the path curves left and zigzags steeply downhill, finally descending steps to a track. Turn left, at a fork take the right hand track and almost immediately, at a Gordon Way post, turn right onto a path which bends sharply left and continues uphill through dark and gloomy conifers.

On the next stage of the walk you need to look out for the regular Gordon Way posts as the winding path is difficult to follow at times but it eventually reaches a track. Cross it, keep ahead steeply uphill to emerge from the trees and continue across open moorland to the triangulation pillar on the summit of Knock Saul Ⓑ. At a height of 1351ft (412m), this is another superb viewpoint, with extensive vistas over the Don valley and Grampian Highlands.

From here retrace your steps to the start, taking care on the descent through the forest, looking out for the frequent waymarked posts and enjoying more fine views on the latter stages over Suie Hill.

Banchory, River Dee and Crathes Castle

Start	Banchory
Distance	$8\frac{1}{2}$ miles (13.7km)
Approximate time	4 hours
Parking	Banchory, Bellfield car park off Dee Street
Refreshments	Pubs and cafés at Banchory, restaurant at the Milton complex, restaurant at Crathes Castle
Ordnance Survey maps	Landrangers 38 (Aberdeen, Inverurie & Pitmedden) and 45 (Stonehaven & Banchory), Pathfinder 258, NO69/79 (Banchory)

A splendid walk beside the River Dee downstream from Banchory, using a former railway track, is followed by a short circuit of the superb wooded grounds of Crathes Castle. The castle is well worth a visit and the circuit includes a gentle and easy climb to a magnificent viewpoint overlooking the Dee valley. After leaving the castle grounds, you retrace your steps along the disused railway track, enjoying more fine views.

At the far end of the car park, go through into a grassy picnic area, bear right across it, go through a fence gap and turn left along a tree-lined, tarmac track. Bear slightly left at a junction of tracks and keep ahead – now along a rough track – passing to the left of a house.

The track bears right, bears left by a hotel entrance and continues beside the high wall bordering the hotel grounds. Where it curves left again, immediately turn right through a fence gap and turn right again along a tarmac path. Take the right-hand path at a fork and continue through parkland beside the River Dee, curving left to a junction. Turn right along a short section of tarmac track and the route then continues along a rough, tree-lined track, formerly part of the old Deeside railway line which ran from Aberdeen to Ballater.

The track keeps in a straight line – sometimes close to the river and sometimes parallel to the road – for almost $2\frac{1}{2}$ miles (4km) to finally emerge onto the road Ⓐ by the entrance to the Milton complex, which comprises a restaurant, craft and art galleries, pottery, countrywear shop and fly fishing centre. Keep along the road and turn left along the drive to Crathes Castle.

Just after passing the lodge gates, bear left onto a path, signposted to Castle, which keeps along the right edge of conifer woodland parallel to the drive, following a white-waymarked route. Look out for where a white arrow

Crathes Castle

directs you to turn right B up to the drive, cross it and keep ahead gently uphill through trees. Bear left on joining another path and continue uphill to rejoin the drive. Keep along it, curving right into the car park, and turn left along a tarmac track, passing the castle ticket office, to the visitor centre, shop and restaurant.

For over four centuries Crathes Castle was the home of the Burnett family but now belongs to the National Trust for Scotland. It is a superb example of a 16th-century tower house, modernised and made more comfortable over the centuries, and is surrounded by colourful gardens and extensive wooded grounds. The interior retains some of its original painted ceilings.

Continue along a path past the restaurant to a sign 'Start of Viewpoint and North Trails' and keep ahead into woodland, following a pink-waymarked trail. At a fork, take the right-hand path which winds gently uphill, crosses another path and keeps ahead to a

magnificent viewpoint over the Dee valley C. From this viewpoint, turn left, now on a blue-waymarked trail, onto a path which turns right, descends steps and then turns left to continue downhill through trees. Cross a track and keep ahead across grass to join a tarmac path at a fork by the castle.

Turn sharp right along the path signposted 'East Trail and Main Gate Path' which bears left gently downhill into woodland again. At a yellow- and white-waymarked post, turn right down steps and continue along a path – now on a white route again – to a T-junction. Turn left along the right inside edge of trees, keep ahead on joining a track and after crossing another track, you rejoin the outward route B.

Retrace your steps to the castle entrance and then walk back along the disused railway track to Banchory.

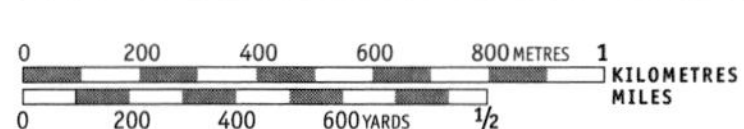

SCALE 1:25000 or 2½ INCHES to 1 MILE 4CM to 1KM

Bunzeach Forest

Start	Bellabeg, car park and picnic area just to west of war memorial
Distance	11½ miles (18.3km)
Approximate time	5 hours
Parking	Bellabeg
Refreshments	None
Ordnance Survey maps	Landranger 37 (Strathdon), Pathfinders 227, NJ21/31 (Strathdon) and 243, NJ20/30 (Cock Bridge)

Most of this lengthy but relatively easy walk is on wide, well-surfaced and well-waymarked forest tracks, used by cyclists as well as walkers. The rest is along quiet, narrow lanes. Much of the route is through conifer forest but at the beginning and end, and at the approximate half-way stage, fine views open up over the lonely countryside of Strathdon and the surrounding hills.

River Don at Bellabeg

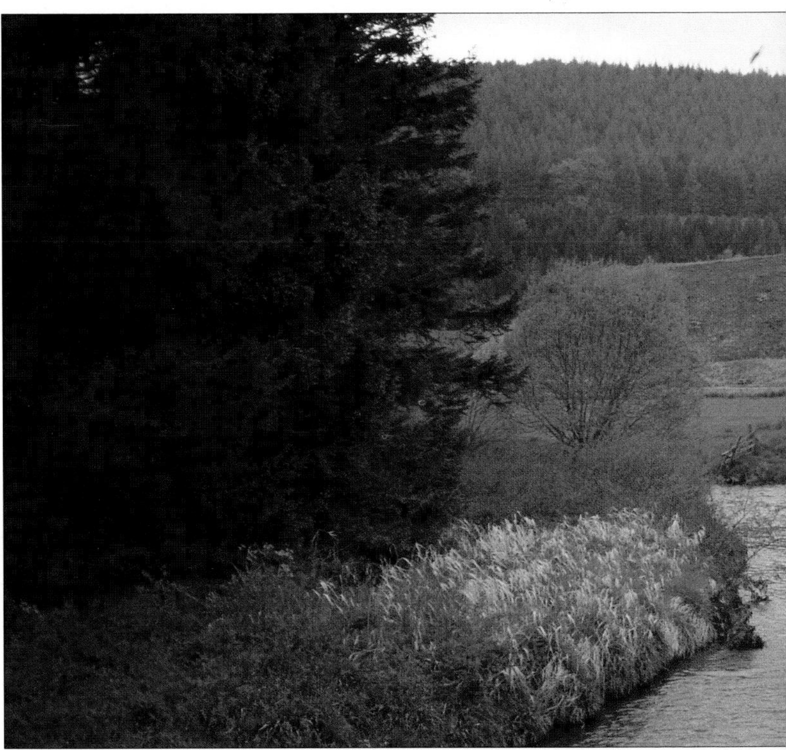

On the other side of the road from the car park there is a motte, all that remains of the 'Doune of Inverochty', the principal fortress in this region until the construction of the powerful medieval castle at Kildrummy. Begin by turning right out of the car park and just before the bridge over the Water of Nochty, turn right down a lane signposted to Strathdon church. Cross the bridge over the River Don and continue along the winding lane, passing the handsome Victorian estate church, to a T-junction. Turn left and after about 200 yards (183m), Ⓐ bear slightly right and pass beside a barrier to walk along a track, following a green-waymarked trail. Keep along this winding track – there are several sharp bends – for the next 2¾ miles (4.4km), initially along the left edge of the trees and later through the conifers of Bunzeach Forest. The forest gets its name from Craig of Bunzeach, one of the hills within its confines. It was mostly planted between 1950 and 1970 and mainly comprises pine, larch and spruce.

Keep on the main track all the while, heading gently uphill most of the time, to eventually reach a T-junction Ⓑ. Turn right – now on a blue- and red-waymarked route – to continue through the forest, heading downhill and finally bending sharp left and continuing down to a T-junction on the edge of the trees Ⓒ. Ahead is a felled area. Turn left along a straight track which, after passing beside a barrier, heads up to a farm. It bends first right and then left to pass to the right of the farm buildings – beyond which it becomes a lane – and you continue along this narrow, winding lane for almost 1 mile (1.6km), as far as the corner of conifer woodland on the right Ⓓ.

Turn left here along the track to Tillyduke Farm and at a fork, take the

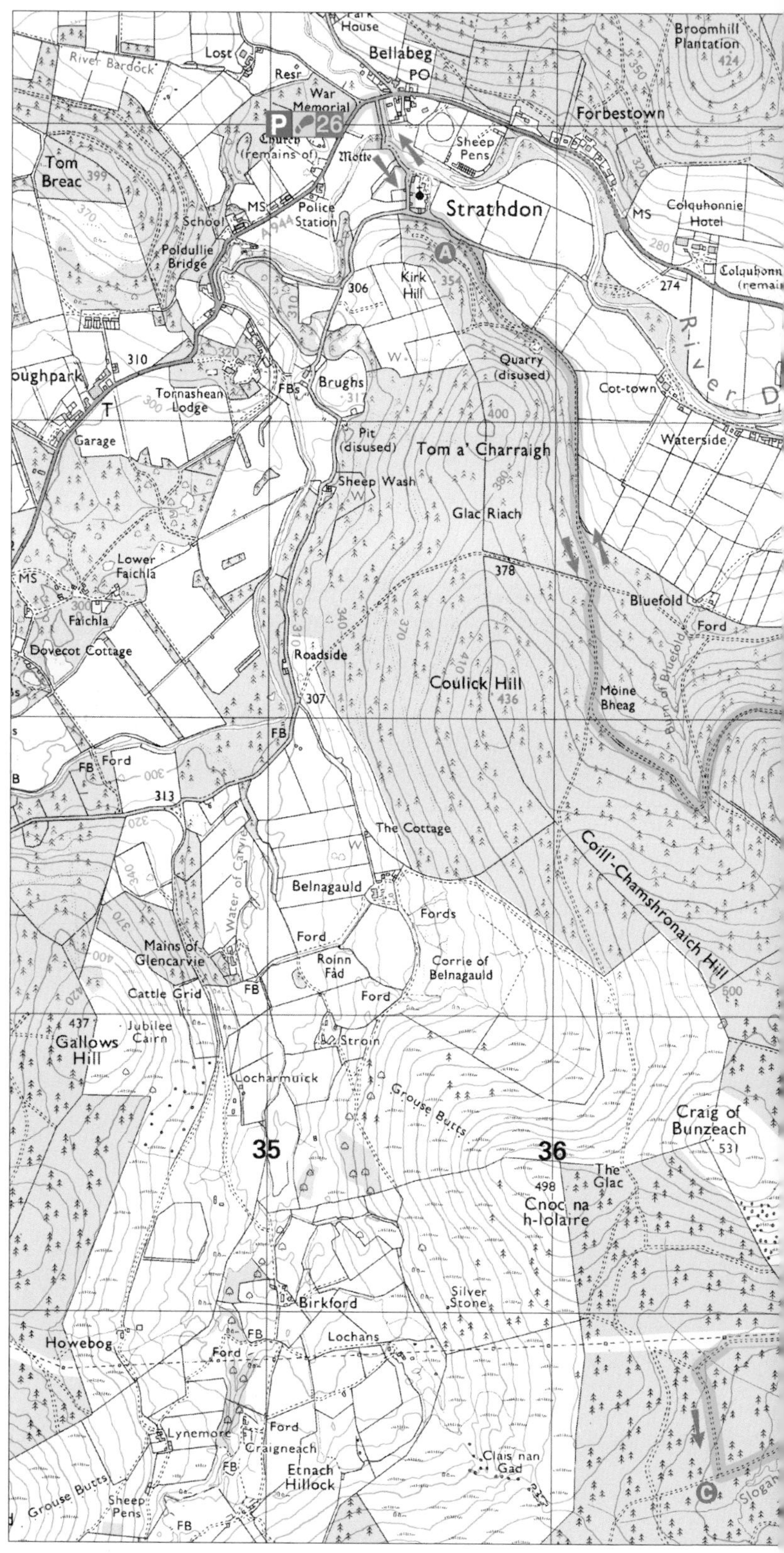
Park House
Broomhill Plantation
424
Lost
Bellabeg
River Bardock
Resr
PO
War Memorial
26
Church (remains of)
Motte
Sheep Pens
Forbestown
Tom Breac
399
370
MS
Police Station
Strathdon
School
A944
MS
Colquhonnie Hotel
Poldullie Bridge
A
280
Colquhonn (remai
306
Kirk Hill
354
274
310
River D
310
320
Quarry (disused)
oughpark
Tornashean Lodge
FBs
Brughs
317
Cot-town
300
T
400
Pit (disused)
Waterside
Garage
Tom a' Charraigh
Sheep Wash
380
Glac Riach
Lower Faichla
378
MS
Bluefold
300
Faichla
Ford
Dovecot Cottage
Burn of Bluefold
340
370
410
Roadside
Coulick Hill
Moine Bheag
436
307
FB
Ford
FB
300
313
320
The Cottage
Coill'-Chamshronaich Hill
340
Water of Carvie
Belnagauld
370
Fords
Mains of Glencarvie
Ford
400
Roinn Fàd
Corrie of Belnagauld
420
Cattle Grid
FB
Ford
500
437
Jubilee Cairn
Gallows Hill
Stroin
Locharmuick
Grouse Butts
Craig of Bunzeach
35
36
531
The Glac
498
Cnoc na h-Iolaire
Silver Stone
Birkford
Howebog
FB
Ford
Lochans
Ford
Lynemore
Craigneach
FB
Etnach Hillock
Clais nan Gad
C
Slogan
Grouse Butts
Sheep Pens
FB

right-hand track to pass beside a barrier and re-enter the forest. Head gently uphill – following a green-waymarked route for the rest of the walk – and then head down to a T-junction Ⓔ. Turn left uphill again and take the first turning on the right Ⓑ. Here you pick up the outward route and retrace your steps to the start.

0 200 400 600 800 METRES 1 KILOMETRES
0 200 400 600 YARDS ½ MILES

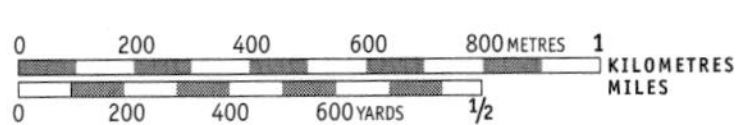

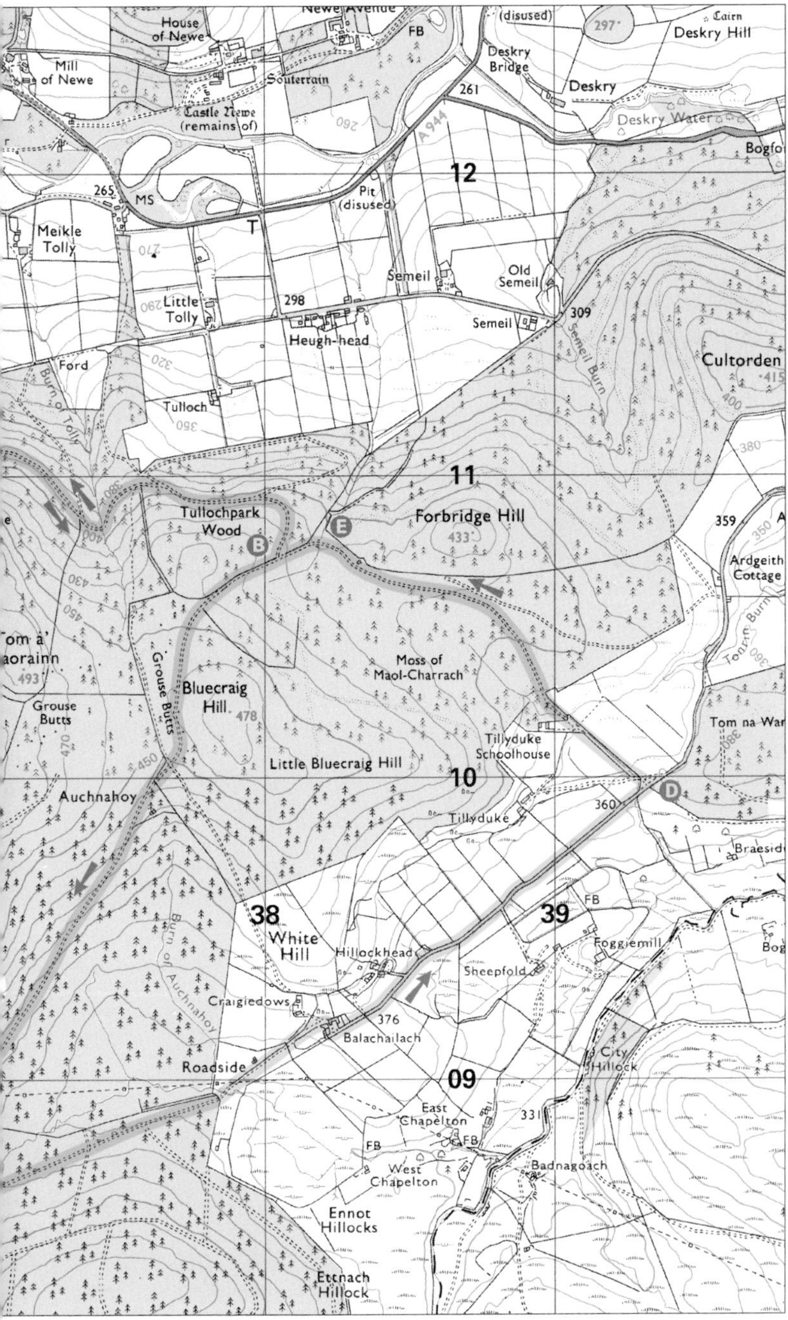

SCALE 1:25 000 or 2½ INCHES to 1 MILE *4CM to 1KM*

Clachnaben

Start	Glen Dye, car park on west side of B974 about ½ mile (0.8km) north of Bridge of Dye and 1½ miles (2.4km) south of junction with road to Aboyne
Distance	6 miles (9.7km)
Approximate time	3½ hours
Parking	Glen Dye
Refreshments	None
Ordnance Survey maps	Landranger 45 (Stonehaven & Banchory), Pathfinder 272, NO68/78 (Glen Dye & Glenbervie)

After an opening stretch through attractive woodland, you emerge into open country and the main objective of the walk, the large and distinctive rocky crown on the top of Clachnaben, immediately comes into view. It remains in view for the rest of the way as you make your way up a clear and well-surfaced path, finally swinging left and heading more steeply up to the 1932-ft (589-m) summit. The views from here are superb. The climb is steady rather than strenuous; simply take your time, pause to admire the views and enjoy it. This walk is not recommended in bad weather, especially in wintry or misty conditions, unless experienced in walking in such conditions and able to navigate by using a compass.

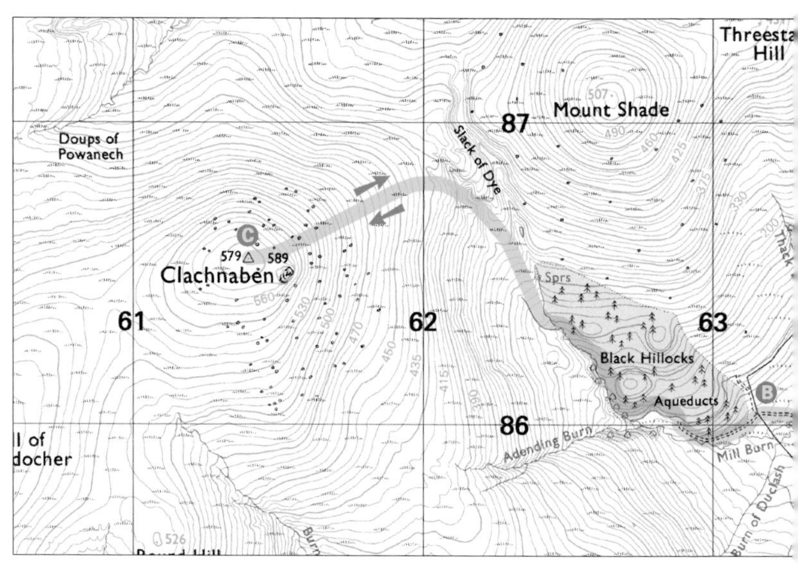

Take the path, signposted to Clachnaben and Glen Dye, which leads off from the car park and heads uphill through woodland. It later descends to a crossroads and you keep ahead along the right edge of trees to a stile. To the right is a fine view of the distinctive rocky crown of Clachnaben.

After climbing the stile, keep ahead to cross a bridge over a burn and at the fork ahead, take the right hand track Ⓐ. At the next fork, take the right-hand track again to continue up the glen, crossing three small burns – all with footbridges – and making for the block of conifer woodland ahead. Climb a stile in front of the trees Ⓑ and continue along the path ahead which initially heads into them but then continues uphill – quite steeply at times – along the left edge of the wood above a burn.

Clachnaben

At the corner of the wood, continue uphill along a clear and well-surfaced path – climbing steps in places – which curves left and heads more steeply up to the rocky summit Ⓒ. The views from here over hills and forests are magnificent.

From here retrace your steps downhill to the start, enjoying more fine views over Glen Dye.

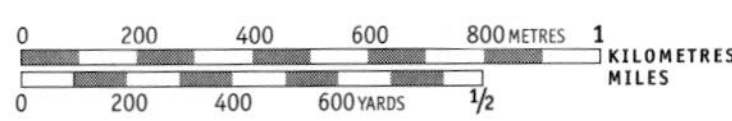

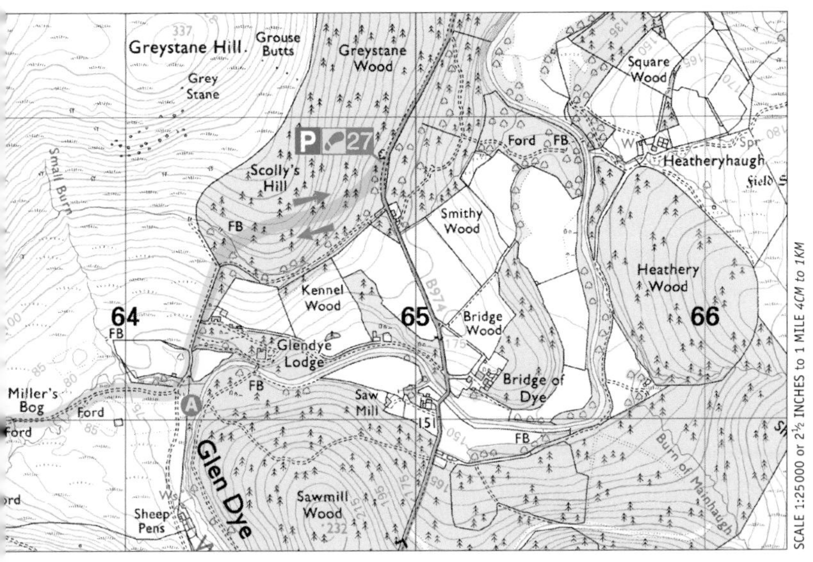

Mither Tap, Oxen Craig and Craigshannoch

Start	Bennachie Centre, on minor road between Chapel of Garioch and Monymusk
Distance	9 miles (14.5km). Shorter version 6½ miles (10.5km)
Approximate time	5½ hours (4 hours for shorter walk)
Parking	Bennachie Centre
Refreshments	None
Ordnance Survey maps	Landranger 38 (Aberdeen, Inverurie & Pitmedden), Pathfinder 214, NJ62/72 (Inverurie & Insch).

The prominent landmark of Bennachie, one of the most easterly outposts of the Grampian Highlands, rises above the Don valley and is dominated by the conical rocky outcrop of Mither Tap. The first and last parts of the walk are through the delightful woodlands that surround the hill; the middle section is across the heathery moorland on the hilltop and takes in the three rocky summits of Mither Tap, Oxen Craig (the highest point) and Craigshannoch. This is a most exhilarating and enjoyable walk of tremendous views and great variety and, although the initial climb to Mither Tap is quite steep, the remainder of the route is relatively undemanding. The short walk goes over Mither Tap but omits the other two summits. This walk is not recommended in bad weather, especially in winter or in mist, unless experienced in walking in such conditions and able to navigate by using a compass.

The walk begins at the information board just in front of the Bennachie Centre and the first part of it follows Gordon Way signs. Turn left along a track which initially keeps by the left inside edge of the trees and then continues through the forest, gently rising to a fork. Take the right-hand track which heads up to a T-junction and turn left onto a path.

The path winds gently uphill to a track where you turn left. At a footpath post turn right along a path to another T-junction Ⓐ, turn right and after a few yards, turn right again – here leaving the Gordon Way – onto a path which heads uphill, across an area of heather, gorse and scattered trees, towards the distinctive summit of Mither Tap. The ascent is initially relatively gentle but it then becomes steeper and rockier and the final stretch to reach the base of the rocky summit cone is across open moorland.

At a fork just below the summit, bear left along the base of the cone –

following pale green waymarks – take the right-hand path at the next fork and climb steps to a footpath post and T-junction Ⓑ. The main route continues to the left but if you want to climb to the summit or if you are doing the shorter walk, turn right at the T-junction, turn left at the next footpath post and turn right at the next post, curving right around the base of the cone in order to climb it from the north. The views from the summit, 1698ft (518m) high, are magnificent and there are also the remains of an Iron Age hillfort.

If doing the shorter walk, turn left – before climbing to the top – at a sign to Rowantree along a clear descending path and rejoin the full walk where a path comes in from the left Ⓔ.

For the full walk, return to the T-junction Ⓑ. The full walk follows an orange-waymarked route from the T-junction, heading downhill and snaking across the heathery moorland to a crossroads. Turn left here onto a path which winds up to the more gentle slopes and less pronounced rocky summit of Oxen Craig Ⓒ. At 1733ft (529m), this is the highest point on Bennachie and, not surprisingly, is another superb viewpoint.

At a footpath post near the top, turn right along the narrow ridge and the path starts to descend, curving right to a footpath post by a large boulder (Little Oxen Craig) Ⓓ. Turn right, in the Craigshannoch direction, and head gently uphill, curving left over the rocky flanks of Craigshannoch – still on an orange route – to a footpath post. Turn right, continue across the

Mither Tap

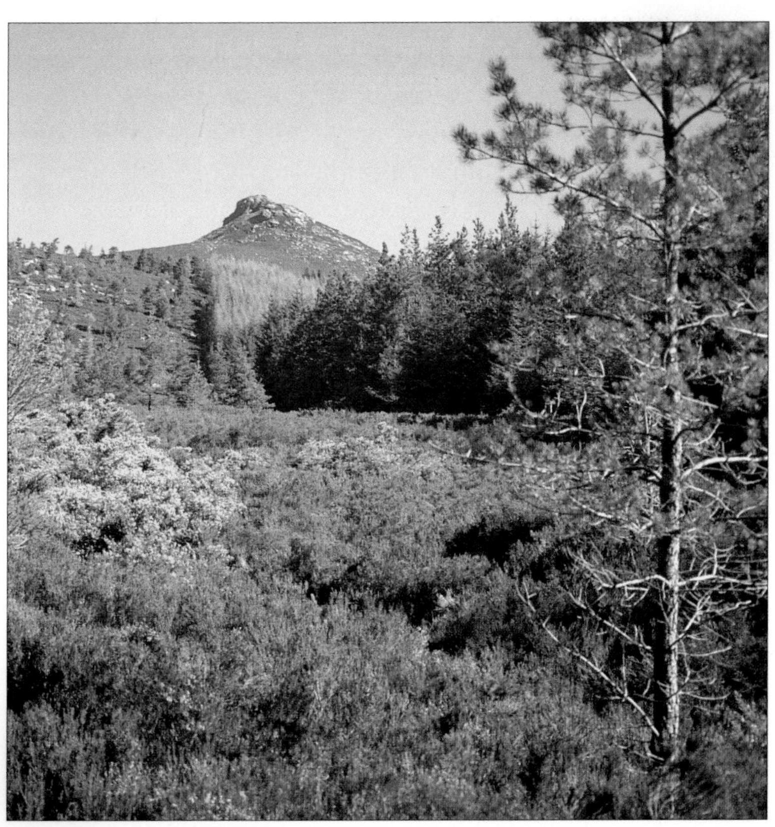

moorland towards Mither Tap but at a fork, take the left-hand path, signposted to Rowan Tree car park. The winding path heads downhill to a T-junction E where you rejoin the shorter route.

Turn left and continue downhill along a path called the Maiden Causeway, across moorland and through woodland, to a crossroads of paths F. This is about 200 yards (183m) before descending to the car park. Turn right, at the next crossroads turn left downhill and the path curves right to continue – now as a wider track

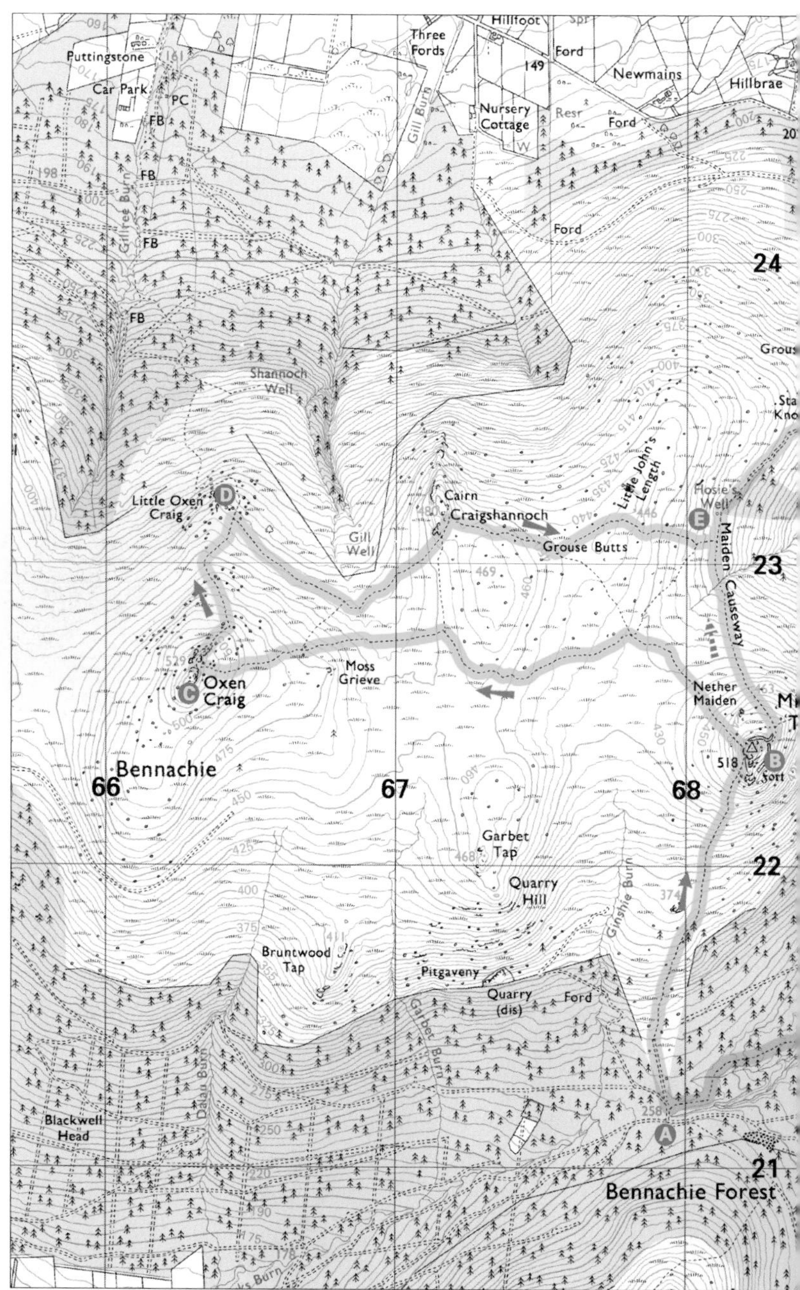

– along the left edge of woodland. Continue along this pleasant undulating track – sometimes along the left edge of the trees and at other times through them – to a T-junction. Turn left and the route keeps along a straight track by the left edge of woodland.

Where the track turns left, keep ahead along a path to re-enter woodland and continue as far as a crossroads G. Turn left along a path which leads back to the Bennachie Centre.

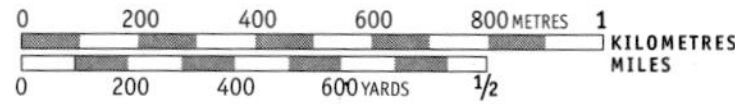

SCALE 1:25 000 or 2½ INCHES to 1 MILE *4CM to 1KM*

Further Information

The Law and Tradition as they affect Walking in Scotland

Walkers following the routes given in this book should not run into problems, but it is as well to know something about the law as it affects access, and also something of the traditions which can be quite different in Scotland from elsewhere in Britain. Most of this is common sense, observing the country code and having consideration for other people and their activities which, after all, may be their livelihood.

It is often said that there is no law of trespass in Scotland. In fact there is, but the trespass itself is not usually a criminal offence. You can be asked to leave any property, and technically 'reasonable force' may be used to obtain your compliance – though the term is not defined! You can be charged with causing damage due to the trespass, but this would be hard to establish if you were just walking on open, wild, hilly country where, whatever the law, in practice there has been a long tradition of free access for recreational walking – something both the Scottish Landowners' Federation and the Mountaineering Council of Scotland do not want to see changed.

There are certain restrictions. Walkers should obey the country code and seasonal restrictions arising from lambing or stalking. Where there is any likelihood of such restrictions this is mentioned in the text and visitors are asked to comply. When camping, use a campsite. Camp fires should not be lit; they are a danger to moorland and forest, and really not necessary as lightweight and efficient stoves are now available.

Many of the walks in this book are on rights of way. The watchdog on rights of way in Scotland is the Scottish Rights of Way Society (SRWS), who maintain details on all established cases and will, if need be, contest attempted closures. They produce a booklet on the Scottish legal position (Rights of Way, A Guide to the Law in Scotland, 1991), and their green signposts are a familiar sight by many footpaths and tracks, indicating the lines of historic routes.

In Scotland rights of way are not marked on Ordnance Survey maps as is the case south of the border. It was not felt necessary to show these as such on the maps – a further reflection of the freedom to roam that is enjoyed in Scotland. So a path on a map is no indication of a right of way, and many paths and tracks of great use to walkers were built by estates as stalking paths or for private access. While you may traverse such paths, taking due care to avoid damage to property and the natural environment, you should obey restricted access notices and leave if asked to do so.

The only established rights of way are those where a court case has resulted in a legal judgment, but there are thousands of other 'claimed' rights of way. Local planning authorities have a duty to protect rights of way – no easy task with limited resources. Many attempts at closing claimed rights of way have been successfully contested in the courts by the Scottish Rights of Way Society and local authorities.

A dog on a lead or under control may also be taken on a right of way. There is little chance of meeting a free-range solitary bull on any of the walks. Any herds seen are not likely to be dairy cattle, but all cows can be inquisitive and may approach walkers, especially if they have a dog. Dogs running among stock may be shot on the spot; this is not draconian legislation but a desperate attempt to stop sheep and lambs being harmed, driven to panic or lost, sometimes with fatal results. Any practical points or restrictions applicable will be made in the text. If there is no comment it can be assumed that the route carries no real restrictions.

Scotland in fact likes to keep everything

as natural as possible, so, for instance, waymarking is kept to a minimum (the Scottish Rights of Way Society signposts and Forest Walk markers are in unobtrusive colours). In Scotland people are asked to 'walk softly in the wilderness, to take nothing except photographs, and leave nothing except footprints' - which is better than any law.

Scotland's Hills and Mountains: a Concordat on Access

This remarkable agreement was published early in 1996 and is likely to have considerable influence on walkers' rights in Scotland in the future. The signatories include organisations which have formerly been at odds - the Scottish Landowners' Federation and the Ramblers' Association, for example. However they joined with others to make the Access Forum (a full list of signatories is detailed below). The RSPB (who hold much of the high ground of the Cairngorm plateau) and the National Trust for Scotland (the new owners of the Mar Lodge Estate) did not sign the Concordat initially but it is hoped that they will support its principles.

The signatories of the Concordat are:

Association of Deer Management Groups
Convention of Scottish Local Authorities
Mountaineering Council of Scotland
National Farmers' Union of Scotland
Ramblers' Association Scotland
Scottish Countryside Activities Council
Scottish Landowners' Federation
Scottish Natural Heritage
Scottish Sports Association
Scottish Sports Council

They agreed that the basis of access to the hills for the purposes of informal recreation should be:

River Dee near Balmoral

Freedom of access exercised with responsibility and subject to reasonable constraints for management and conservation purposes.

Acceptance by visitors of the needs of land management, and understanding of how this sustains the livelihood, culture and community interests of those who live and work in the hills.

Acceptance by land managers of the public's expectation of having access to the hills.

Acknowledgment of a common interest in the natural beauty and special qualities

Glossary of Gaelic Names

Many of the place-names in Scotland are Gaelic in origin, and this list gives some of the more common elements, which will allow readers to understand otherwise meaningless words and appreciate the relationship between place-names and landscape features. Place-names often have variant spellings, and the more common of these are given here.

aber	mouth of loch, river
abhainn	river
allt	stream
auch, ach	field
bal, bail, baile	town, homestead
bàn	white, fair, pale
bealach	hill pass
beg, beag	small
ben, beinn	hill
bhuidhe	yellow
blar	plain
brae, braigh	upper slope, steepening
breac	speckled
cairn	pile of stones, often marking a summit
cam	crooked
càrn	cairn, cairn-shaped hill
caol, kyle	strait
ceann, ken, kin	head
cil, kil	church, cell
clach	stone
clachan	small village
cnoc	hill, knoll, knock
coille, killie	wood
corrie, coire, choire	mountain hollow
craig, creag	cliff, crag
crannog, crannag	man-made island
dàl, dail	field, flat
damh	stag
dearg	red
druim, drum	long ridge
dubh, dhu	black, dark
dùn	hill fort
eas	waterfall
eilean	island
eilidh	hind
eòin, eun	bird
fionn	white
fraoch	heather
gabhar, ghabhar, gobhar	goat
garbh	rough
geal	white
ghlas, glas	grey
gleann, glen	narrow, valley
gorm	blue, green
inbhir, inver	confluence
inch, inis, innis	island, meadow by river
lag, laggan	hollow
làrach	old site
làirig	pass
leac	slab
liath	grey
loch	lake
lochan	small loch
màm	pass, rise
maol	bald-shaped top
monadh	upland, moor
mór, mor(e)	big
odhar, odhair	dun-coloured
rhu, rubha	point
ruadh	red, brown
sgòr, sgòrr, sgùrr	pointed
sron	nose
stob	pointed
strath	valley (broader than glen)
tarsuinn	traverse, across
tom	hillock (rounded)
tòrr	hillock (more rugged)
tulloch, tulach	knoll
uisge	water, river

of Scotland's hills, and the need to work together for their protection and enhancement.

The Forum point out that the success of the Concordat will depend on all who manage or visit the hills acting on these four principles. In addition, the parties to the Concordat will promote good practice in the form of:

- Courtesy and consideration at a personal level.
- A welcome to visitors.
- Making advice readily available on the ground or in advance.
- Better information about the uplands and hill land uses through education.
- Respect by visitors for the welfare needs of livestock and wildlife.

- Adherence to relevant codes and standards of good practice by visitors and land managers alike.

Any local restrictions on access should be essential for the needs of management, should be fully explained, and be for the minimum period and area required.

Queries should be addressed to:
Access Forum Secretariat, c/o Recreation and Access Branch,
Scottish Natural Heritage, 2 Anderson Place, Edinburgh EH6 5NP.

Safety on the Hills

The hills, mountains and moorlands of Britain, though of modest height compared with those in many other countries, need to be treated with respect. Friendly and inviting in good weather, they can quickly be transformed into wet, misty, windswept and potentially dangerous areas of wilderness in bad weather. Even on an outwardly fine and settled summer day, conditions can rapidly deteriorate at high altitudes and, in winter, even more so.

Therefore it is advisable always to take both warm and waterproof clothing, sufficient nourishing food, a hot drink, first-aid kit, torch and whistle. Wear suitable footwear, ie. strong walking boots or shoes that give a good grip over rocky terrain and on slippery slopes. Try to obtain a local weather forecast and bear it in mind before you start. Do not be afraid to abandon your proposed route and return to your starting point in the event of a sudden and unexpected deterioration in the weather. Do not go alone and allow enough time to finish the walk well before nightfall.

Most of the walks described in this book do not venture into remote wilderness areas and will be safe to do, given due care and respect, at any time

Dunnottar Castle at dawn

of year in all but the most unreasonable weather. Indeed, a crisp, fine winter day often provides perfect walking conditions, with firm ground underfoot and a clarity that is not possible to achieve in the other seasons of the year. A few walks, however, are suitable only for reasonably fit and experienced walkers and should definitely not be tackled during the winter months or in bad weather, especially high winds and mist. These are indicated in the general description that precedes each of the walks.

Mountain Rescue

In case of emergency the standard procedure is to dial 999 and ask for the police who will assess and deal with the situation.

First, however, render first aid as required and make sure that the casualty is made warm and comfortable. The distress signal (six flashes/whistle-blasts, repeated at intervals of one minute) may bring help from other walkers in the area. Write down essential details: exact location (six-figure grid reference), time of accident, numbers involved, details of any injuries sustained, steps already taken; then despatch a messenger to phone the police.

If leaving the casualty alone, mark the site with an eye-catching object. Be patient; waiting for help can seem interminable.

Useful Organisations

Association for the Protection of Rural Scotland
Gladstone's Land, 3rd floor, 483 Lawnmarket, Edinburgh EH1 2NT.
Tel. 0131 225 7012

Forestry Commission
Information Branch, 231 Corstorphine Road, Edinburgh EH12 7AT.
Tel. 0131 334 0303

Historic Scotland
Longmore House, Salisbury Place, Edinburgh EH9 1SH. Tel. 0131 668 8600

Long Distance Walkers' Association
21 Upcroft, Berkshire, SL4 3NH.

National Trust for Scotland
5 Charlotte Square, Edinburgh EH2 4DU. Tel. 0131 226 5922

Ordnance Survey
Romsey Road, Southampton SO16 4GU.
Tel. 08456 05 05 05 (Lo-call)

Ramblers' Association (Scotland)
Kingfisher House, Auld Mart Business Park, Milnathort, Kinross KY13 9DA.
Tel. 01577 861222

Royal Society for the Protection of Birds
Abernethy Forest Reserve, Forest Lodge, Nethybridge, Inverness-shire PH25 3EF.
Tel. 01479 821409

Scottish Natural Heritage
Information and Library Services, 2/5 Anderson Place, Edinburgh EH6 5NP.
Tel. 0131 554 9797

Scottish Rights of Way Society Ltd
John Cotton Business Centre, 10/2 Sunnyside, Edinburgh EH7 5RA.
Tel. 0131 652 2937

Scottish Wildlife Trust
25 Johnston Terrace, Edinburgh EH1 2NH. Tel. 0131 226 4602

Scottish Youth Hostels Association
7 Glebe Crescent, Stirling FK8 2JA.
Tel. 01786 51181

Tourist Information Centres
Aberdeen and Grampian Tourist Board:
Tel. 01224 632727
Highlands of Scotland Tourist Board:
Tel. 01997 421160
Local tourist information numbers:
Aberdeen: 01224 632727
Ballater: 013397 55306
Banchory: 01330 822000